The author has been telling tales all of his life that he can recall, some of them tall and some of them less so. Originally planned a career in the film industry by way of a rather disastrous university course; he fell from scripts to novels and thought he would try his luck in the literary world. This, of course, was like giving up on Mount Kilimanjaro and deciding to just go straight for Everest instead. Always dreaming but never hopeless, he hopes to bring smiles to a few faces wherever he can.

To anyone who has ever told me that I could do this, and even to anyone who said that I couldn't, as it motivated me all the same. To all the good people in my life, you know who you are.

Scott Richards

THE LEGEND OF PAPER MONKEY

AUSTIN MACAULEY PUBLISHERS™

LONDON • CAMBRIDGE • NEW YORK • SHARJAH

A CIP catalogue record for this title is available from the British Library.

ISBN 9781398403697 (Paperback)
ISBN 9781398403703 (ePub e-book)

www.austinmacauley.com

First Published (2021)
Austin Macauley Publishers Ltd
25 Canada Square
Canary Wharf
London
E14 5LQ

Thanks to all at Austin Macauley for making my first publishing experience a smooth ride.

Chapter One

Johnny Rocket had only ever wanted to be one thing. A rock star. He had the fortunate name. He had the love of music. He had the desire. He had the leathers. Unfortunately, the only thing Johnny lacked was the only thing he actually needed.

Talent. He wasn't just average. He wasn't even just plain old bad. Johnny occupied a level on the musical ability spectrum that was all his own. Had he been trained by a combined team of Mozart, Elvis and Hendrix, he still would have been rubbish.

There's a famous lyric that mentions guitars gently weeping. In Johnny's case, the poor instrument would have a nervous breakdown every time he picked it up. One thing he didn't lack though was heart. Misplaced though it may have been, Johnny believed it was his destiny to be a rock star. Sometimes one should never question the power of desire over ability, and Johnny had a big gap to make up for.

It was the day of Johnny's twenty-seventh birthday, and as he awoke, he had an epiphany. It might have been due to the fact he had heard his step-father telling his mother it was about time he moved out, or, seeing as he was such a glass half full sort of guy, it might have been the dream he'd had about his sell-out world tour. Either way, Johnny's belief that morning was even stronger than normal.

He followed his set routine, taking a swig of Jack Daniels as he believed all rockers did first thing. He then set himself a line of what he had been told was cocaine, but in all probability was talcum powder. Not that he knew the difference.

A few minutes later, he bounded down the stairs, his whistle wet and his right nostril as soft as a baby's bottom. His mother had been kind enough though to leave him a now cold cup of tea which was propping up a birthday card.

Johnny didn't have time for birthdays though. He had rehearsals planned with his band, Paper Monkey. Johnny had never explained to anyone why he had chosen the name for the band. He thought this gave him an air of creative mystery like people would assume he knew something that they didn't. Of course, in most cases where Johnny was concerned, the opposite was true.

Before leaving the house, he checked himself in the mirror. Big hair, check. Leather jacket, check. Skinny jeans, check. He pulled a pair of oversized sunglasses from his jacket pocket and slid them over his nose. Check. Satisfied that he looked the part, he left the house and began wandering down the street in full daydream mode.

Every time Johnny walked down the street it was an exercise in spatial awareness. Johnny would be slowly pacing, his head firmly stuck in the clouds, whilst the young, old and infirm alike all bounced off of him without him really noticing. Someone could have pulled a gun and shot him (and a few people over the years had given serious consideration to that very thought) but he wouldn't have felt it, he would have carried on his merry way, humming whatever melody was swirling around his mind at the time.

Soon enough, he arrived at his friend Baz's house. Johnny was greeted at the door by the lively, plump figure that was Becky, the 'better half' of Baz. Ushering him into the kitchen, she proudly showed him the birthday cake that she had spent all morning baking in anticipation of his visit.

"You shouldn't have Becks, you daft bird."

"Oh don't be silly, Johnny. It is your birthday."

Bounding into the Kitchen came Baz, bald, boisterous and built like a bear.

"Happy birthday, kid!" He embraced Johnny in a hug so crushing that it could have turned coal into diamond.

Feeling for his ribs, Johnny wheezed a thank you.

Baz threw Johnny a can of lager.

"I'm cancelling band today, mate. Seeing as it's your birthday."

"Cancelling? Since when?"

"Well, like I said, it's your birthday. Plus, Joe and Sponge can't make it. Got work."

Joe and Sponge were the other two members of the band. Bass guitarist and drummer respectively, they were, rather ironically in terms of usual band dynamics, the talented ones. Neither of them cared that much about making decent music though, what they did enjoy was getting hammered which, being in a band of any sort presents lots of opportunities to do so.

"I thought we were going to go over the set for the gig on Friday," Johnny found himself whining a little.

"We will. Tomorrow. Besides, we'll just be doing the usual anyway."

The 'usual' was an hour-long set at the local pub, The Brunswick Cross. The landlord, known locally as Buster Head, was an old friend of Johnny's long-gone dad and felt some responsibility to look after him. Sentimental though he was, he also was not an idiot. Paper Monkey's set occurred with coincidental regularity at the same time as happy hour. Punters were far more receptive to music that was half as good as they expected in their local as long as they were getting twice as much alcohol as they were paying for.

Johnny took a thoughtful slurp of his premium strength supermarket lager.

"I've been thinking, Baz."

"You have?" Baz had known Johnny for a long time and Johnny starting a sentence with 'I'm thinking' never ended well.

"Maybe we should start looking at other venues."

Baz and Becky exchanged glances. This conversation reared its unrealistic head every few months, and the two were running out of excuses to let Johnny down gently.

The problem was, Baz knew the band were terrible. The only reason he stayed was out of loyalty. He never expected them to go anywhere.

"I dunno John. Buster tells me he's got a few important people coming this Friday, if you know what I mean."

Johnny perked up instantly, "Really?"

"That's what Buster said."

This was in fact true. What Baz selectively failed to mention to his friend though was that the 'important' people Buster had been talking about were the council health inspectors, who had heard rumours about the kitchen at the

Brunswick that would require the intervention of dragon slayers, never mind pest control.

"Did they say what record company they were from?"

"No, not really mate. They did mention though that they were on the lookout for something…new." New, in this case, being a breed of cockroach usually only found in the most dense of rainforest floors, but as was so often the case in Johnny's life, ignorance was bliss.

"Fantastic…maybe I'll play that new track that I've been working on."

Baz and Becky found themselves exchanging that look again.

"Which track would that be John? I don't think Baz has mentioned it," Becky was sugar-coating her words even more than her deserts. The reason Baz hadn't mentioned it was for the sole reason that when Johnny had given him a demo he had truly felt like giving himself a double Van Gough. No more ears, no more pain.

Johnny felt a swell of pride as he prepared to eulogise about his masterpiece.

"It's called Th—"

In a seemingly cosmic intervention that Baz and Becky were simultaneously grateful for, the phone rang. Both leapt up, but it was Baz, in true bear style, who snatched up the handset like a grizzly fishing a salmon from a lake.

"Hell-o?" A puzzled look spread over Baz's face, the kind he normally only showed when the local Chinese ran out of spare ribs.

He thrust the phone Johnny's way.

"Hell-o? Oh alright, Buster. Cancelled? You have? That's fantastic. Thanks, mate."

Johnny handed back the phone and smiled like a dog who had finally caught his tail.

"Friday's gig at the arms is cancelled. Something about health inspectors."

Baz attempted to conceal his delight for the sake of his friend.

"Oh, that's a shame mate. Suppose we'll just to have a piss up won't we?"

"Oh, we will. Afterwards."

"After what?"

"Buster's only gone and got us a gig at the student union. We're actually gonna play in front of people who still have their own teeth!"

"How did he…manage that?"

"Apparently, the bar manager there owes him money or something."

Baz attempted to hide his newfound hatred for Buster.

"Wow, that's…I'm speechless mate." Baz was far from speechless, but nothing that could have been mentioned before the watershed.

"I know what you mean. This could be our big break Baz. Best birthday present ever!"

Baz and Becky communally realised that quashing Johnny's dream about a big break, especially on the day of his birthday would be akin to posting a letter to every child in the country on Christmas Eve telling them the only fat man coming down their chimney that night was the local burglar. Still, Baz could only worry. Sure, the entire audience would still be heavily intoxicated. Which is good for any band, and was quadruple true for a 'band' like Paper Monkey. Yet they were also students. This meant they would be young, and tuned in to the Zeitgeist. Whether this meant they recognised good music from bad wasn't the point, but Baz was pretty sure that the audience would *think* they knew what good music was, and in his mind that only spelt trouble. Then again, maybe they could turn it to their advantage. Perhaps they could be one of those bands that became known as great due to the sheer fact of how fantastically shit they actually were. Baz stared down into his beer can. He had got far too used to grasping at straws where Johnny was concerned.

"Well, John, I'll give the others a ding, see if they can get out of work early. We'd better get rehearsing."

Somewhere not too far away, another young man was rehearsing. His name was Alberto Pablez. He focused on the English language textbook in front as he vainly tried to ignore his homesickness. Peru to England was a long way, and a few months into the term he was really starting to feel it. Not that the people around him weren't doing their best to help him fit in. It was just that he was used to certain rituals that he no longer had to conform to. Ironically, those were the very rituals and traditions that he had sought to escape by coming to one of the more obscure Universities in England.

It was at this point that one of his flatmates knocked on the door.

"It's open."

In walked Laura, who was very sweet and had her heart in the right place but Alberto was struggling to separate the fine line between friendly and patronising.

"Hey, Alberto! You up to much tonight?"

"I...must study my English."

"Bollocks. You're coming with us."

Alberto flipped through his book of translations but could find no reference to these 'bollocks'. He assumed it was some sort of colloquialism with reference to livestock. What this had to do with his social life though, he could never interpret.

"I really must study, Laura."

"No, you really must relax a bit, Al."

"Al?"

"It's something I'm going with, work with me. Anyway, there's this band playing the S.U. tonight, apparently, they're like nothing that's played before." (This was true, but not necessarily a compliment.)

"Oh…well, I probably won't like that type of music."

"Well, I thought you'd say that. Which is why I bought you this flyer."

She threw a piece of paper in his direction, it sat lightly in the air for a moment before floating down onto the desk, an A5 feather of destiny.

He held it in front of him and squinted at the bold letters that were emblazoned across the top.

"Paper Monkey?"

"That's right."

"Is this meant to be funny?"

"What? No, I just thought…"

"Thought what? Let's have a laugh at the funny talking foreign man because this band has the same name as the God of his local village? Har-har!"

"You…you're taking this the wrong way, Al."

"My name is Alberto. Now I would like to carry on with my work please."

As he watched the girl stomp out of his room, Alberto turned his attention back to his studies. Yet there was something that was suddenly gnawing at his stomach. He felt an odd sensation that he had upset Laura and that by upsetting her, he had also upset himself a little. He tried to shake off the feeling. He stared again at the flyer.

Just seeing the words Paper Monkey, he felt a flood of memories rush in.

Alberto was from a tiny little village that had for centuries worshipped a God which translated into English was 'Paper Monkey'. Hence why Alberto believed that the others were just making fun of him. The gig started at nine. He had been studying a lot lately…maybe he would have a look, he thought, just to see what this 'Paper Monkey' sounded like.

Johnny stepped out onto the stage as though he were a gladiator entering the coliseum. Strutting out onto the sticky student union stage was hardly entertaining at the jewel of the Roman empire but for Johnny this felt just as epic, with just slightly less chance of someone taking a swing at him with a sharp blade. His eyes gazed across the room that would be soon full of cheap booze induced drunken appreciation. Deluded as he was, even Johnny had come to realise that his gigs tended to go a lot better where copious amounts of alcohol were involved. He took a deep breath and envisaged the night ahead. Running onto the stage, whipping the crowd into a frenzy…hopefully have some underwear thrown at him. He would take a dirty pair of kickers as a rock trophy at that point. He definitely had a feeling though. Tonight was going to be the turning point. Tonight was going to be special.

Tonight was going to be—

"John! Get your daydreaming arse out here and grab some gear!" Baz yelled from behind an open fire exit from which they were bringing in their instruments, amps and equipment.

John took another look from the stage. As he turned to go and help out, he saw a girl approaching from the other end of the room. She swept a lock of dark brown hair out of her left eye as she came up to the stage.

"You're Johnny, right?"

Johnny felt a swell of pride. His first groupie.

"That's me."

"This is a bit forward but…do you think you can do me a favour?"

Chapter Two

Alberto stepped nervously into the quickly filling room. He wasn't used to crowds, and he didn't like to drink so the student union really wasn't his type of place. Something though had drawn him here. It had occurred to him that even though he had come to England to broaden his horizons he had spent most of the time in his room, moaning to himself about how he was not fitting in with the others. It had dawned on Alberto though that the people around him had made far more effort with him than he had with them.

Squeezing his way to the bar, he prepared to fully initiate himself. As the barman approached, he took a deep breath and readied himself for the test ahead.

"One snake-bite and black please."

Alberto stared down into the red frothy liquid. Now or never. Closing his eyes and saying a silent prayer to the Paper Monkey, he took his first swig.

Half an hour later, Johnny Rocket was in the middle of his set and absolutely loving it. He had blasted through several of his 'hits', such as 'Lubricate my love', 'Harold had a metro' and Baz's own personal favourite, 'Ballad of the salad dodger'.

The crowd was going wild. Well, he assumed it was. A crowd had never gone wild for him before. From the general motion of shouting and jumping, he assumed that they were all having a good time. At the very least, none of them appeared to be having a bad time.

Pausing after the ridiculously long guitar solo that ended off salad dodger, Johnny grabbed the microphone and addressed the crowd.

"Thank you! This next track…is for a man named Alberto."

Somewhere in the crowd, that very same young man was swinging his t-shirt around his head and chanting something in his native tongue. Of course, nothing evokes excitement in a drunken crowd like a bit of nudity, and quite soon there were dozens of shirts spinning around heads. Johnny, of course, was loving this. He would have preferred that more of the girls were lifting their tops, but beggars can't be choosers. As he launched into one of his new tracks called 'Jelly (should never be eaten raw)' he was pleased to see a bra whiz past his head. This enjoyment was tempered however when, upon tracking the flight trajectory of said bra the launch pad appeared to be the rather fearsome bosom of one of the university rugby players, joined by his teammates in a bout of woman's clothing fancy dress. Why the men's rugby team seemed to be so aggressively concerned with their manhood and yet fully committed to regularly wearing women's clothing was an unsolved mystery on campus.

As the band continued to play, somewhere in the crowd Laura navigated her way through to Alberto, half-naked torsos showing the way like big sweaty cat's eyes.

"Alberto!"

"Laura!"

"Are you alright?"

Alberto shouted something into the ether that was drowned out by Johnny's use of the WA-WA pedal.

"What?"

"I said I am never better. You look a little tense. Have a drink."

"Alberto, are you drunk?"

"I'm not sure. When you're drunk, does the room spin round and you constantly feel as though you might vomit at any time?"

"Pretty much, yea."

"In that case, Laura, I think I may be, what's the expression you used before, pissed as a fart?"

Laura was taken aback a little. She hadn't seen Alberto so much as a look at drink so far. Come to think of it, she hadn't heard him swear either. Not in English at any rate.

Before she could do anything further, the delicately dressed rugby lads had hoisted Alberto up onto their collective shoulders and were parading him around like a trophy.

Laura watched on in horror as Alberto's insides suddenly decided they felt like a day trip and made a fast exit into the outside world. At that moment in time, it transpired that there was a more fearsome sight than half-naked cross-dressing drunken rugby players; half-naked cross-dressing rugby players covered in vomit.

Up on stage, Johnny knew trouble was coming. If there was one thing he had the experience of when it came to his music and a public arena, it was spontaneous outbreaks of violence. Exchanging a quick glance with the others, they all made that special nod that said let's get the fuck out of dodge. With a remarkable speed that had come with far too much practice of exiting a gig at short notice, the band and their equipment were soon nowhere to be seen. Not that anyone on the dance floor had noticed all that much. The occupants of that space were now split into four factions: those inciting violence, those participating in violence, those trying to escape, and lastly those trying to escape but participating anyway (not necessarily by choice).

Laura, who had taken shelter next to the knocked out form of a rather large prop forward, scanned the floor for any sign of Alberto, who had managed to crawl his way through the chaos and was making his way to a fire exit. Laura, following the same exit strategy, soon caught up with him outside on the car park.

"Al, you know all those times I tried to make you drink and you wouldn't?"

"Yes?"

"I think I appreciate why you said no."

Wincing at the sounds emanating from within the building, Johnny and the others bundled their gear into the van. Seeing two figures tumble through a fire exit that looked slightly familiar, he went over to say thanks for coming, seeing as he didn't really get the chance to say it on stage.

Laura rolled her eyes as she saw him coming over. The last thing she wanted to deal with now was some horny rocker looking for a quickie in the back of his van. Then again, she reminded herself, he had helped her out.

"Well," said Johnny, addressing Alberto. "I don't think I need to ask if you enjoyed yourself."

Alberto smiled and swayed slightly. Johnny moved away from the angle of more vomit on instinct.

"And you?"

"Yea it was fun. Up to a point."

"So you like the tunes?" Johnny asked, aiming for cool but only achieving creepy.

". Look, Johnny, If you think just because you did me a favour then I owe you anything then you can take your guitar and stick …"

Johnny stepped back and waved his hands in peace. "No, no! I just, well I never get much feedback. Well not positive feedback anyway."

"Well, good then. I suppose I didn't hate them." Laura replied, throwing the smallest of bones. "Is the rioting normal though?"

Johnny thought on this for a moment. "It's not totally unheard of. Well thanks for coming anyway, but I better get going myself. After parties and all that."

"Sure. Well. Bye. Oh, and thanks for the mention. I think Al really appreciated it, didn't you Al?"

"I want a kebab," said Al, trying to put one foot in front of the other.

"I think that's a yes. C'mon Al, let's get you back," said Laura, dragging the drunken South American by his arm.

"Are we getting a kebab?" Al asked, eyes wide and ready for more new 'experiences'.

"No," Laura replied as firmly as she could, whilst trying not to sound too much like her own mother.

"Why? I really want a kebab."

"That's only because you've never had one before. Trust me. There are some parts of our culture you really do not want to sample."

Back in the van, Johnny was trying hard not to sulk.

"She was supposed to be my first groupie. She was not supposed to be going home with a pissed up Mexican kid."

Now when a friend says something like that, the typical response is to say something reassuring along the lines of 'You can do better'.

Johnny's band mates though knew that this probably wasn't true.

"Ah well," said Baz. "You'll catch her at the next gig I bet."

"Yea mate," piped in Sponge. "Probs playin' hard to get. And I think he was Peruvian."

"You know what, you pedantic git, you're probably right." Said Johnny, The great thing about Johnny was that, due to his unfounded belief in things turning out well for himself, he was very easy to pick up when down. It was a necessary survival skill that he had developed over the years.

A by-product of this belief meant that on extremely rare occasions, Johnny had something of a brainwave. At that point in time, on the back of that bus, the universe had chosen to imbibe Johnny with the seed of a brilliant idea. After all, the universe probably assumed that Johnny would mess up the idea and then it could pass it on to somebody useful. For whatever reason though, this time, things were different. This time the idea wormed is way to the front of Johnny's brain and said 'UP HERE DUMMY!'

Johnny bolted forward in the back of the van.

"Shit!"

"What's up, Johnny?" Asked Baz. "Acid reflux again? I've told you about those bloody snakebites."

"I-I've just had an idea." Johnny spoke quietly, slightly spooked by his own thoughts.

The rest of the band did a silent, collective 'uh-oh'.

"Joe, turn the bus around." Johnny asked.

"Why? Bloody hell, Johnny, we'll be home, can't you just piss in a bottle like you normally do?"

"I don't want the toilet. I need to see that Mex— the puking kid. This is important. Just turn us around, please?"

Baz sighed. The missus was going to kill him.

"Go on, Joe. Back to the Uni. This better be good, John."

Baz was always the most tolerant of Johnny's mad schemes, though his patience was always stretched when he knew that supper was waiting.

This was better than good, thought Johnny. He pulled out a battered notebook from his pocket and flicked through the pages. About a month ago, he had this image stuck in his head. This symbol. A symbol he had drawn again and again for days until it faded from his mind. That was until Alberto had removed his shirt. Johnny had been too wrapped up in the gig to notice at the time, but it had come to him on the bus, he had noticed that Alberto had a funny tattoo running down his shoulder. A funny tattoo that looked a lot like the funny drawings in his notebook...

Back in his room, Alberto was currently worshipping the god of porcelain.

Laura stood outside the toilet. "Al...you okay?"

"I think so. I think my body has run out of things to..." There was a pause as he searched for an English phrase that seemed appropriate. "Expel."

He meekly crept out and made his way into the kitchen, his ears ringing and his stomach-churning.

Pouring him a glass of water, Laura sat down next to him at the kitchen table.

"You should drink this."

Al glanced at the glass as though it were marked with a skull and crossbones.

"Perhaps later."

A quiet fell around them, interrupted only by pained gurgling from the young Peruvian's belly.

That was until a light tap-tapping presented itself from the kitchen window.

Laura wondered who it could be. Could a member of the rugby team be looking for revenge? No, she thought. They wouldn't have bothered to knock. That left only one person really.

Laura clenched her teeth and pulled back the curtain.

"What do you want, Johnny?"

"Hi. I er…, I just thought I'd check if Alberto was okay. I do feel responsible. A little bit. A really tiny bit actually."

"I get the picture. He'll be fine."

"Oh right. Cool."

Johnny shuffled his feet slightly. Despite Laura's obvious resistance to him being there, he persisted on.

"I don't suppose I could have a chat with him?"

"About what?"

"His tattoo actually. Look, if it makes you feel any better I am not trying to get into your knickers. Unless you want me to of course."

After a look from Laura that if couldn't kill, would certainly result in a lengthy stay in the hospital, Johnny realised that was not the way to go.

"Look, I can see you're a little protective of your pal, but I just want to have a chat with him. Scouts' honour."

"You were in the scouts?"

"No, but I do look good in a sash and I'm great with knots."

He saw the giggle try to dig its way under the barbed wire fence of Laura's stubbornness.

"Was that a smile?"

Laura gave up. "I'll open the door."

Soon after, Johnny was sat in the kitchen, along with Alberto and a very suspicious Laura.

"So, Al. You like being called Al, right?"

"No."

"Oh," clocking the smirk on Laura's face from the corner of his eye, Johnny carried on regardless.

"So I noticed you have a tattoo."

"It is tribal. A rite of passage for all men in my village."

"Cool. Right," Johnny had experienced many so-called 'rites of passage'. Seeing as most of these had ended up with him waking up either in a cell or a hospital, he assumed that Alberto had gone through something different altogether.

"Why are you so interested in my tattoo?"

"I'm a creative person. Musician, artist, thinker I take a keen interest in symbolism."

Alberto afforded himself a sigh. It felt like he had been explaining the tattoo ever since he had stepped off the plane.

"It is a symbol of our faith."

"In the paper monkey god?"

27

"He is *not* a monkey. It just doesn't translate too well. It is hard to explain. It is easier to break it down. Paper is used to create, right? To write, to draw to paint. It is a blank slate for creation. And what does a god do? A god gives life. He creates."

Johnny processed this information, noting to self that the kid was quite hammered. Still, it did make some kind of sense. Then again Johnny realised, seeing as he himself were quite far from sober, it was bound to.

"I get you," said Johnny. "So where does the monkey come in exactly?"

"Well, paper comes from trees, which themselves are a symbol of ever-growing life."

A light bulb flashed somewhere above Johnny's head. "And monkeys climb trees!"

"Exactly. Have you heard enough? I'm pretty sure I'm going to vomit again. Soon."

"Yea I think I'm done. Just do me a favour when you've finished chucking. Have a look at these."

He tossed a couple of torn pages toward Alberto and made his way to the door, promptly followed by Laura, who went not to so much see him out but just to make sure out was where he was headed.

"What was all that about, really? I don't buy that creative crap you gave as an excuse," Laura tried not to wince as the sound of her own voice bounced around her head. She really was turning into her mother.

"No offence, but I don't care. Tell me something though. Do you believe in destiny?"

"No."

"Didn't think so. But think about this, you're the one who brought Al into my world. You asked me for the favour. Think about why that happened."

Laura knew why it had happened. She just wasn't going to admit it to anyone.

"Bad judgement on my part."

Johnny smirked. The happy smirk of those who think they are on to something other than the wrong path for once.

"Ha. Well, you believe that. Night," with that, he pushed his sunglasses up onto his nose and strode out into the night. Then, realising he couldn't see a damn thing, slid them back down again.

That night Johnny didn't have any dreams about groupies on tour buses or chucking TVs out of windows. In fact, he had the best night's sleep he could remember having since before he used to have dreams of that sort. This might have been down to the fact that he was really tired. It might have been down to the fact that he had stayed off of the talcum powder that night. When he awoke the next day though he told himself that it was something else.

Whatever bizarre coincidences had occurred the previous night, had ignited something within him. He felt that he didn't need to dream anymore because now something was happening. Something special. He just didn't know what it was yet.

Alberto was sat back at his desk, wide awake. A desk light shone its beam on a few crumpled pieces of paper that he just could not take his eyes off of. Rolling up his left sleeve, he stared at his tattoo, and then back at the paper. It was impossible. None of this made any sense. As he tracked the tattoo around his arm with his finger, he couldn't help but wince as every touch of the needle came back in tiny little stabs of memory He then thought back even further, admiring his father's tattoo and wondering when he would get his own. All the children would gather around a large open fire, eyes wide in wonder and mouths agape as one of the village elders would tell them tales of the past, and the importance of their tribal God. La Leyenda de Mono de Papel. The Legend of Paper Monkey.

The old man would delight in spinning his tales, telling the children that fables as old as the village foretold how one day a son born under the light of the Paper Monkey would one day meet the spirit, trapped in human flesh.

Alberto snapped himself back into the present, staring once again at the drawings on the paper.

He had never believed in the stories of the old men. Not that he wasn't proud of his heritage, he just found it unlikely that the protective spirit of their village would choose to wander around the earth wearing a man's skin. Especially the skin of Johnny. Still, the pictures were quite compelling evidence. Rational, even. Well, in the context of any of this being rational. Alberto couldn't have drawn them better himself even if he had tried.

Alberto opened his laptop and began typing an email. He needed some advice on what to do with this 'evidence'. He just hoped that those crazy old men were connected to Wi-Fi.

The following morning, Baz, Sponge and Joe sat in Baz's front room, awaiting the usual post-gig debrief.

The strange thing about that particular morning though was that Johnny was a no-show. There were many things that

Johnny was known to be late for, but this wasn't one of them. Joe picked at his Mohawk haircut, whilst Sponge stared blankly at Baz's locked booze cabinet.

Baz fidgeted in his seat. Waiting always made him hungry.

Finally, after several more minutes of playing, staring and fidgeting, in came Johnny. This wasn't the Johnny they all recognised. Well, physically it was. It wasn't as though he turned up wearing a novelty set of glasses complete with big nose and moustache.

Johnny came in that morning with a different air about him. He wasn't the excitable child he normally was at these meetings. Instead, he had a calmness about him. Johnny could tell this worried the band. They were used to a routine.

"Lads, something happened last night."

"I know. We made it over halfway through a set. Think that's a record," Joe's voice was completely empty of sarcasm.

"Apart from that. I think something happened. An epiphany."

This time Sponge answered, his answer just as genuine as his love of anything fermented.

"Epiphany? I think my uncle had one of them. Nasty business. You wanna get that checked out. He didn't walk right for weeks after."

"Not quite the same thing I don't think Sponge."

"Oh."

"So what is this epiphany then, Johnny? I hope it's quick. We're running close to brunch here," Baz gently tapped his stomach to comfort it, as though he was settling a restless new-born.

"Well, it's simple really. After that whole thing with the tattoo last night, it came to me. I know what we were meant to do, as a band. What we have to do," Johnny let his sentence hang in the air for dramatic effect, and to see if anyone was going to throw up a good guess.

"Anyone?" Johnny continued. "Peru, lads, it's obvious! We have to go to Peru!"

Johnny could see that they were all looking at in him in the way they only did when he had been eating mushrooms, and not the kind you put in an omelette.

Sponge was the first to react. "I had a two for one on breakfasts voucher that expired today Johnny. I gave that up hoping that for once you might say something other than total bollocks. You owe me two sausage, two bacon, scrambled egg, black pudding, toast, beans and unlimited refill of tea and coffee. Up to eleven AM." With that, Sponge got up and left, a genuine sadness in his eyes. Joe said nothing, but followed Sponge out in leaving the room.

That left Baz. Good old, reliable Baz. At least he wouldn't be letting him down. He'd back him, even to a different continent.

"Bloody hell Johnny." Baz finally said after far too many empty minutes. "Peru? You've got no fucking chance."

Chapter Three

Somewhere else, another man was thinking about his own destiny. Lee Jones looked out from the window in his top-floor office. He had founded Easy Sell records fifteen years ago, after his own musical career failed, and they had not been an easy fifteen years. He had spent millions of someone else's money trying to find that special something, the band that would redefine music, no, the world forever. His search so far had been fruitless. Every time he thought he had it, his backers would tell him to keep looking. They said he would know. They told him to look for a sign.

Like Johnny though, he had an unfounded belief, a burning desire that had never floundered. That had been backed up by a conversation he'd had recently with his nephew, a university rugby player.

Young Tristan Lee had a habit of trying to sell his uncle on 'the next big thing'. Lee had been about to let him down gently once again until he had heard the name of the band. Wandering around his desk, he smoothed out a crumpled flyer. Reading the words 'Paper Monkey', a disgustingly sly smile crawled across his face. Finally, he thought, this must be it.

A week and quite a lot of booze based convincing later, Johnny and the band found themselves on a train from Birmingham New Street to London Euston. It had been a whirlwind few days, from receiving the phone call to begging the rest of the band to take him seriously. This time he was sure, was the real deal.

"I'm not sure about this, John," Baz's voice was almost lost in the noise of London traffic as the four band members entered out onto the street from the station.

"Look, lads, I've told you, I've got a good feeling about this bloke," Johnny took in the view around him.

Not normally the voice of common sense, Sponge was actually with Johnny on this one. "Well, if the bloke is going to pay us what he said on the phone he's going to pay us, then I'm putting pen to paper."

"You'd sign your left bollock away if you got paid for it, you tight git," came the colourful insight into Sponge's character from Baz.

Sponge didn't argue. "Well, I'd still have a spare," he reasoned.

"We're a cab ride away from living the dream," Johnny said, trying his best to inspire.

Sponge suddenly looked worried. "A cab. In *London?*"

"Don't worry mate," said Johnny. "Mr Jones said all expenses are on him."

He waved at a passing cab.

A well-bartered-for taxi ride later, the band met a record executive for the first time.

Lee might as well have had stereotype tattooed on his forehead. The only thing wider than his shark-like smile was his stomach. Johnny could almost hear the buttons on his designer suit groaning as they held together in a valiant effort against his vast bulk. He was only a tail and some whiskers away from being a literal fat cat.

"Hello, boys. I'm Lee. Lee Jones."

At this point, the syndicate that Johnny's heart had on his choices was in full power and when his brain tried to stand up for itself it ended up with broken kneecaps.

It was this unique biological makeup that allowed Johnny to sit in that office and hold a chloroform soaked cloth over the mouth of his common sense as Lee pushed a fat wedge of papers over the desk toward Johnny. Flashes of Sunday school hit repeat on the projector of Johnny's mind, he remembered something about a snake and an apple. He then remembered that an apple a day was supposed to keep the doctor away and that he shouldn't bother worrying about the small print.

What he did do was take a glance around the office. As expected, there were photos of bands. Oddly enough though, they were all of the same band. A band with a fat lead singer. With a wide smile. The intelligent part of Johnny temporarily took the reins and decided to do some investigating.

"You used to be in a band?"

"I was, as it happens." Lee replied with unearned pride. "You've probably heard of us. The Mad Caps."

"Can't say it rings a bell." Replied Johnny. "Lads?"

A collective shake of band heads confirmed that none of them had heard of the Mad Caps.

"Maybe you're just a little too young. I bet you've heard the single though. Hamsters are my enemy. Got to one hundred and twenty-one in the charts in nineteen-eighty-three."

Johnny and the band looked impressed, though it was only because they didn't know anybody had ever bothered counting the charts that high. Or low, depending which way you were looking at things.

"So what kind of sounds did you chaps produce??" Johnny couldn't help notice that Lee actually had a plaque that read '121 in the top 100, April 1983'. Johnny could appreciate the pride taken in such a minor achievement. After all, it was still better than anything he had ever managed. So far.

"Oh, we had a mixed sound. Kind of new-romantic, reggae, ka, synth-rock. With a touch of jazz fusion. We were heard of our time."

Johnny realised upon this description why he had never heard it. It was because surely any evidence of what sounded like the worst musical idea ever would have been scorched from the earth for the sake of all mankind. And this from the mind of Johnny, a man who once had to be talked down from sampling the mating cry of penguins in a track called 'Waddling for love'.

"Enough about me though. Today is about you. Have a look at the paperwork, think it over, have a talk with your lawyers," Lee had the decency not to stutter or laugh on that last word, even though he could have accurately guessed any lawyers the band had encountered thus far were court-appointed.

"Well, I tell you what," he continued. "I'll sort you out with a company credit card, a nice hotel suite, go out, enjoy the city, sleep on it and we'll meet back up tomorrow. Sound Good?"

Company credit did sound good, especially to Sponge. A band-wide approving nod later, Lee pressed a button on his desk intercom. A universal means of communication between big bosses and secretaries everywhere.

"Susie?"

"Yes, Mr Jones?"

"Why don't you finish early and give the boys the tour."

"Yes, Mr Jones."

Taking his finger away from the intercom, he addressed the band once more.

"Susie will take good care of you. You are about to be rock stars, gentlemen. So go and have a good time. Just try to avoid throwing anything out of a window eh?"

Several hours and multiple flashes of the company credit card later, the majority of the band and a few sudden hangers-on lay sprawled across a swanky hotel suite as suggested, drifting merrily to sleep.

Johnny though did not find himself in slumber's snugly arms. He sat awake, images of a foreign country playing across his tired mind. How was he was supposed to pull this one-off? *Excuse me, I know you've just spontaneously handed us a record deal but could you send us to Peru for reasons I can't explain and barely understand?*

Still, his unwavering faith had led him this far, he had to trust the musical gods were going to see him through. This thought calmed him as drifting off to sleep, he cuddled a bottle of some vintage spirit that was older, and if you blew on the bottle top the right way, actually produced a better sound than he did.

Chapter Four

Lee sat in the office and watched the sunrise. The anxiety in finding the act his South American benefactors had charged him with uncovering, had been replaced with something else. He fidgeted in his chair, unable to find comfort. Something inside was bothering him, scratching away deep below the surface. He stood and surveyed the office. Why was it he had founded the company again? It felt like so long ago that he wasn't sure he even knew the answer anymore. He had wanted to find musical genius…and he certainly hadn't found that. Spending so long consumed with finding this band, he suddenly realised he had no clue what he was supposed to do next.

He pressed the button on his Intercom. No answer. He pressed it again, growing impatient. Where the hell was Susie? A tick-tock from the wall clock grabbed his attention. It's five am, you idiot. She wouldn't be at work for another three hours.

The chair groaned as might a constipated cow as he collapsed back into it. He reached for the bottle of brandy and returned his gaze to the hypnotic hue of the early morning sun as it broke through and cast a million tiny reflections across the glass and steel of the city skyline.

The phone rang. Not the normal phone, but the phone that had just one connection. Direct to them. Lee handled the handset as he might an angry snapping turtle.

"Hello?" Lee always braced himself slightly, even though he had only ever heard the one hiss on the other end of the line.

"You have found the one?"

"Yes. I think so."

"Good, good. You must bring him to us."

"How? I don't know where—"

"We will send full instruction."

With that, the line went dead. Lee replaced the handset, hands trembling. Something felt wrong. Had he been a more spiritual man, he might have said that his soul was itchy.

Johnny awoke to find his three band members peering over him. As firsts sights of the day go, it wasn't the best.

"Wake up, John. We need to talk, all of us," Baz's tone carried a gravity Johnny was not used to hearing.

"Well, we better make it quick. We're supposed to meet Mr Jones at twelve."

"That's the thing, John," this time it was Joe sounding serious. What the hell was wrong with them?

"We've had a chat and we don't want to sign. Even though it's loads of dough." Sponge was the kind of man who counted out his chips to make sure he was getting his monies worth, so Johnny knew something must be serious.

This news shocked Johnny out of his hangover to the point where he leapt out of the bed.

"You don't want to sign? But this is the dream!"

"No, John. This is your dream. Not ours, never was really. For me, it was just…something to do. Besides, the rest of us have real jobs." Joe said, exasperated,

"Jobs, Joe? Jobs? The only jobs you should be concerned about are blowjobs. Which, when we hit it large, will be plentiful," Johnny couldn't think of a better selling point. Unfortunately, the plea fell on deaf ears.

"I have bills to pay John, we all do. I can't pay my rent with promises from some fat bloke I've just met. Have you not thought about why we have never heard of him? Why there was no gold disc on the walls?" This time it was Sponge doing the 'reasoning'.

Johnny felt the anger welling up. What a bloody time to turn on him.

"Oh, c'mon Sponge. You would rather spend your life working for the council?"

"It's an important job! Someone has to make sure the bins get collected on time. And would it be so friggin hard to call me Steve for once?"

Johnny was hoping this was a terrible dream. Not once in his life had he called Sponge Steve, and he was fucking sure he was not going to start now.

"Well…if that's how you all really feel. I'll do this without you. All of you. Oh and *Steeeeeve?* The bin-men. Are. Always. Late."

He stormed out as best a man who has forgotten he slept naked can leave any room. Pausing in the corridor to ponder his nudity problem, Baz came following out, albeit wearing more clothes.

"Look, John, I don't trust that Mr Jones. None of us does. Then there's all that bollocks about Peru. When are you going to mention that? It's too much John, I'm sorry."

"Then why have you stuck with me at all?"

That was a question Baz had been dreading hearing, and the one he was looking forward to answering even less.

"Because…someone needed to. I suppose at one point I'd thought you'd get bored, get a proper job and just, you know…" Baz trailed off. He knew this would be taken about as well as a strawberry shortage at Wimbledon.

"Give up? Well, you obviously don't know me that well. Now if you'll excuse me I have a meeting to go to," Johnny pulled himself together, stuck his pigeon chest out and proceeded to march off down the corridor once more. It was only when he reached the lift, bare buttocks still facing back towards Baz that he said, "Erm, Baz, I don't suppose you've seen my pants anywhere have you?"

Alberto sat in his room, eyeing his half-packed suitcase as though this were all its fault. Did he really want to go back? Tradition was tradition but how was he supposed to learn about the outside world if he went running back home at every sniff of fulfilling the prophecy? On the plus, surely if he did go back he'd be welcomed home as a hero, the local boy who found the Paper Monkey! That's if he was right of course.

Checking his emails, he saw that the elders had indeed been hanging out in the internet café. If Alberto had any doubts, they certainly did not. Their reply was definitive.

'YOU MUST BRING HIM TO US'.

Underneath this, was an added note 'Your mother said to ask whether you are eating enough, and keeping your underwear clean'.

Alberto pondered on his reply, never before had he felt the weight of destiny push down on him so heavily He was almost afraid to look at his tattoo in case it started talking to him. He settled on as simple a reply as he could think of. 'Yes to everything'.

Alberto considered leaving without telling anyone but that just didn't seem right. Besides, he didn't want to leave without saying goodbye, especially to Laura. Well, actually, if he was being honest with himself he didn't want to leave and say goodbye to her at all, but this was all a lot bigger than what he wanted.

Taking a breath, he knocked on her bedroom door.

"It's open, Al," he pushed the door open and stepped inside.

"How did you know it was me?"

"Because you're the only one polite enough to knock."

"I have some, er, bad news. I hope."

"You hope you have bad news?"

"No…I…" Alberto stuttered as he cursed himself for not translating better. He knew what he wanted to say, but he wasn't sure he knew how to say it in his own language, never mind in English. What he meant to say was that leaving her was far harder than he imagined and that he hoped she would feel as bad about him leaving as he did. Not that he wanted to upset her…his mind wandered off. Maybe he didn't know what he wanted to say after all.

"I have to go back home, Laura."

"What!? When, why?" Laura's tone gave him an inkling that perhaps she wouldn't be too keen to see him leave either, but he couldn't be sure. It wasn't as though he had a lot of relationship experience to back up the notion.

"Soon…I…I can't really explain," Alberto watched the expression on Laura's face shift like an angry storm cloud. "Well, maybe I can. I think you're finding it too hard to fit in so you're just going to run away, back to your safe little village."

"No!" he surprised himself with how forceful he sounded. "I am not running…it is…not…I mean it…"

"Isn't your decision?" Laura had gotten used to finishing Alberto's English sentences for him.

"Yes, it isn't," he nearly laughed as even he realised that didn't sound right. "I mean, no it—"

"I know what you meant, Al."

Alberto sucked in a breath. This next bit was really going to make her mad.

"There's something else. You know Johnny…"

Laura's eyebrow arched as though her brain suddenly required a bridge to carry her thoughts from one side to the other.

"What does he have to do with anything?"

"I kind of…need him to come with me."

"What!? Why could you possibly need him to go with you?"

That wasn't an easy one to answer. How was he supposed to tell her that according to the word of an ancient prophecy, Johnny was carrying around the soul of their village God and that as fate had seemingly bought them together it was Alberto's task to bring him to the village?

"Even if we spoke the same language, Laura…there is no way you would understand…"

Laura fell silent for a moment. Then a couple of things clicked into place in her head and she realised just why Alberto was looking so nervous.

"You want me to help you to get him to go with you don't you? So now that you're leaving, you want to use me to help you leave, and convince that idiot how? Am I supposed to seduce him? What is wrong with you!?"

"Like what? No!" It hadn't even crossed Alberto's mind to ask for her help.

"Just get out Al."

"Laura, please—"

Alberto just managed to dodge a desk lamp that made him really question his earlier inkling that Laura may be upset to see him leave.

Alberto stood in the corridor outside trying to work out what the hell had just happened, remembering something his father had said to him the day before he had left. 'Remember son…whatever language you speak…you will never understand a woman's mind…so just accept that they will always be right and make your life a lot easier'. Alberto let out a long sigh. He had told his father at the time that was an old-fashioned load of nonsense, but now he wondered whether his father was a lot wiser than he had given him credit for.

Johnny, now reunited with his leather jacket and skinny jeans, paced round in circles as he tried to come up with a good enough blag to Lee. What was it bands normally said when they had a falling out? 'Creative differences?' Still, he couldn't recall a band breaking up the day after being offered a lucrative record deal. That was one record he really didn't want to hold.

Before Johnny had time to settle on an excuse, the door to the office swung open and there was Lee, looming in the doorway like a stray blimp.

"You seem to be a little light on numbers. I know I said to act like rock stars but…"

"Yea well," it was about all Johnny felt he could manage. "There's only one rock star in that lot. Me."

Moments later, Johnny sat in the office once again, fearing the dream was about to be snatched out from under his feet.

"So let me get this straight, Johnny." Lee put his fingers together as he spoke, an effort that already seemed to cause beads of sweat to form on his far too large forehead. "Yesterday, I offer your band a record deal. More money and opportunity than any of you could ever have dreamed of. Today, you turn up and tell me that the band is no more?"

Johnny looked down, with the look of a school boy who had just ventured 'accidently' into the girls toilets.

"That's the gist, yea." He mumbled.

"Well, that is brilliant news." Lee remarked with a smile.

"It…is?" Johnny, as much as an optimist as he was, didn't have a massive amount of experience in hearing good news.

"Of course. I didn't want to say anything yesterday but it was clear to me after a few seconds that they were all holding you back. You're the one with the talent, Johnny. You're the one who's…special. Destined for a higher purpose."

Though overwhelmed, that did make sense to Johnny. And it was about time someone else recognised his genius.

"So what happens now?" asked Johnny.

"Well, I thought perhaps you and I could take a little trip. Travel broadens the mind you know. Be good for those creative juices, and I could do with a holiday."

"Oh. I thought maybe you'd want me in the studio or something," said Johnny. "I've got enough in my book and in my mush for at least five albums I reckon."

"Plenty of time for that when we get back."

"I suppose…where did you have in mind?"

"Well, Johnny, you know where I've always wanted to go and I hear is absolutely stunning this time of year?"

Johnny felt his heart skip a beat. If the next word that came out of Lee's mouth was 'Peru' than he was either going to soil himself or pass out.

Lee's mouth began to open, in slow motion, it seemed to Johnny. Then the letters winged out of his fat mouth and bore themselves into the air.

"Peru."

"Peru. Right. Peru."

"So what do you think, Johnny?"

"I think you'd better tell me where the toilets are."

An extended period in a cubicle later, Johnny found himself wandering the streets. He had always wanted to get to this point. A record deal. Someone who believed in his talent. But now what? He'd always assumed that the band would be behind him. After all, if a TV was thrown out of a hotel window and there was no band there to see it would it even make a noise? Then there was Peru. It seemed that everywhere he turned Peru was in his face, but why? As he pondered on this, his phone rang. It seemed Peru was not only in his face but in his ear as well.

"Is that Johnny?"

"Yea."

"It's Alberto."

"Bloody hell. You're about to mention Peru aren't you?"

"How did you know?" Alberto asked.

"Well I think the Peru tourist board must have been working there arses off lately because the whole worlds gone mad for Peru."

"Yes well…I can't really explain this but I'm going back and I need you to come with me."

Johnny said nothing but hung up. Was there anyone who didn't want to take him to Peru? Looking back at the last few days, he realised for once, the folly in his previous Peru based enthusiasm. It might have been only a few days ago but it felt like an age. What had he been thinking? Standing there talking about epiphanies, telling his friends that they should go to Peru? For so long he had believed in destiny and now destiny had taken an interest in him yet Johnny suddenly felt lost. Maybe the band had been right, this was all too big for them. They should probably just stick to happy hour at the local. He didn't even like warm weather all that much. It didn't go too well with skinny jeans. He would have to travel with an industrial amount of Vaseline. He'd have hoped that fate could lead him somewhere with a mild climate. Then again…Johnny's inner belief floated to the surface like a lifebuoy of optimism. He had made it this far on a guitar string wing and many a prayer. Might as well see it through. His phone rang again.

"Johnny?"

"I can't go with you to Peru Al, I'm already going. Although I suppose it wouldn't hurt to have a local onboard. My Peruvian isn't the best."

"We speak Spanish, well mostly. My village speaks a mixture of local—"

"Same difference," Johnny cut in. "So you onboard?"

"Onboard what?"

"Do you want the job?"

"Oh. Yes. Thank you."

"Right then. I'll be in touch."

Johnny hung up once more. Bugger it. If destiny wanted him in Peru, then to Peru he would go.

Chapter Five

Alberto had been gone a few days, and Laura was trying her hardest not to mope. Despite his colloquial struggles, he had been one of the few people she could actually have a conversation with. Why should she even care? It wasn't her fault that he hadn't had the bottle to stick it out. And to go to the other side of the world with that idiot Johnny? It just made no sense. If she was going to go travelling, it was because she wanted to grow as a person, not some hunch based on a tattoo. Destiny, who believed in destiny in the twenty-first century?

All these thoughts jostled for position in her brain as she leafed through a book she'd just happened to come across in the uni library. The fact that it was called 'Tribal beliefs and rituals of South America' was irrelevant. There was nothing wrong in a bit of reading, was there? No, she told herself, as she looked in the index for references to a 'Paper Monkey' god. She wasn't concerned about Alberto at all. Not her, no way. Not even a little. The five other books and seven open windows on her laptop all on Peru and ancient Incan culture were a total coincidence.

Baz couldn't enjoy his lunch. This was worrying for two reasons, one it was his favourite, Becky's lasagne. Second, he had never not enjoyed a meal before. Even the dinners at school.

"You're worried about Johnny aren't you?"

"No."

"Liar."

Becky was right. He was worried. He'd been watching out for Johnny ever since he'd known him. There had been many people over the years that had had a lot of negative things to say about Johnny, but he'd always had heart, always stood up for what he believed in. Plus, Baz had always felt bad that Johnny had grown up without a real dad, and had done his best to plug some of the gap.

Still, Johnny was a grown man. Perhaps he'd been looking out for him too long.

Baz took a sorrowful look at the contents of his plate. All this deep thinking had no place at the dinner table. Something else that Baz felt didn't belong at the table was interruptions, so when the buzz of the doorbell cut through his mental processing he was not too pleased.

Becky was not too pleased either when she answered the door to a younger, thinner woman who was asking for 'Johnny's guitarist'.

Still engaged in mental torment and a staring contest with his lasagne, Baz at first didn't take much notice as Becky escorted Laura inside.

"This girl says she's a friend of Johnny's."

Baz managed to break his gaze away.

"I remember you. The groupie."

"I am not a…!"

Laura calmed herself down before she finished the sentence the way she normally would have finished that sentence. She handed Baz a book.

"Turn to page ninety-eight, paragraph three."

Baz, whose literature normally did not expand much beyond takeaway menus, found himself doing as he was told. Laura stood and watched as Baz scanned the page, then looked up, his face suddenly pale and his appetite taking even more of a back seat.

"Bloody hell. You better look at this."

He handed the book over to Becky, who read the same words that Baz had just read. These words:

"In a small area of southern Peru, there exist two tribes who have a centuries-old duel concerning their worshipped God, roughly translated into English as 'The Paper Monkey'.

"Each tribe believes one day a man who contains the spirit of the Paper Monkey will return to them. The village to the east of the river believes the Paper Monkey will bring in an age of peace and prosperity. The village to the west, however, believe that he will crush all enemies, starting with the village to the east. It is believed that the feud began when the western village stripped an old Inca temple of its gold and resources, which the Easterners took as a sign of heresy. Each firstborn son on the East is tattooed with an image of the Paper Monkey and sent out to travel. It is believed that the spirit of the Paper Monkey will be drawn to the tattoo, and the son of the east shall then return home.

"The West believes that it will be an outsider, who under the influence of their Inca gold will return the Paper Monkey to them. The West also believe the only way to free the Paper Monkey is to sacrifice its human host and release the spirit."

Becky finished reading and echoed her boyfriends' sentiments.

"Bloody hell."

"I can't believe it. Johnny was right." Baz was stunned. He couldn't recall ever saying that before.

"What!? No. Johnny was not right," Laura looked at the shocked faces of Baz and Becky and reigned herself in once again.

"What I mean is, I don't think that Johnny is some incarnation of an old Incan god. But those villagers probably will. Which, if this is true means he could be in trouble."

A moment of silence followed. The kind of silence which people normally need after they have just come to learn something absurdly bizarre and bizarrely absurd.

Of course, there are many ways to break a silence. A cautious question. A well-timed, comic breaking of wind. Baz, however, deciding to go for something in between. He chuckled. Not a throaty roar of laughter, nor a mournful, singular 'ha'. He chuckled as might someone who whilst falling off a cliff, remembered an old joke that always made them smile.

"It's typical Johnny. He can't just have a normal destiny, oh no. Has to do things the hard way. There must be someone we can tell. The police?"

"Oh, yea. I'll just phone nine-nine-nine and ask for the special Peruvian ancient ritual prevention squad shall I?" Laura regretted the sarcasm as soon as she let it escape her mouth.

Shrugging off the remark, Baz went on.

"You know earlier, I was thinking that maybe I'd been too protective of Johnny. Now I feel like I haven't been protective enough."

He glanced at Becky, who in act of couple telepathy said 'I'll go and dig out your passport'.

After Becky disappeared upstairs, Laura suddenly felt quite awkward. After all, she had barged in on two strangers having their dinner, and she hadn't exactly been at her most polite.

"Sorry for snapping."

"Don't worry about it. You should hear what comes out of Becky's mouth when she's on a diet."

Realising she didn't know how to respond, Baz followed up with, "It's alright to make a fat joke when you're both on the big side."

"It is?"

"Well, as long as she doesn't hear me. So you got a bit of a thing for him then?"

"Johnny? God no!"

"I meant the Peruvian kid."

"Oh. Maybe...I, well, I don't know. I don't think there's much of a precedent for what to do when you feel like you're getting close to someone and they decide to bugger off to thousands of miles away."

"I'll take that as a yes. You know a flight down there won't be cheap."

"Well, I've got savings for a rainy day. And I've already looked on backpacker chat rooms to find the best route there."

"Well, it seems like you have it all planned out. I should speak to Joe and Sponge, but I think I know what they'll say."

Later, as Baz faced the gaping, cognition free stares of Joe and Sponge, he could at least congratulate himself on a correct prediction.

"I can't believe…" started Joe, "that you believe all that stuff just 'cus it's in a book."

"I agree, Baz," spoke Sponge. "I mean, if we believed everything written down, I'd be a Christian, Muslim, Jewish, Buddhist boy wizard. And that would be a metaphysical and conceptual nightmare."

"I'm not saying I believe the spiritual aspect of it, you pair of dickheads." Baz shot back. "I'm saying if those tribal blokes believe it Johnny could end up kebabbed anyway. Do you really want to let that happen?"

"He'll be fine!" Sponge sounded quite sure. "Probably end up fronting some Peruvian rock-flute band or something. Then they can look after him."

Thousands of miles and a hemisphere away, Johnny stepped out of the small plane and felt the humid hand of fate slap against his cheek, totally unaware of the fuss his trip was causing back home.

It had been a long couple of flights, and the heat and close air were certainly not ingredients that mixed well with his outfit, as he had predicted. Still, he was handling the heat better than Lee, who from the looks of things was attempting to turn sweating into an Olympic sport. At least all the time spent travelling together now meant Johnny now longer felt the need to keep calling him 'Mr Jones'.

"You alright, Lee?"

"Fine, fine." He dabbed frantically at his forehead with a handkerchief, a handkerchief that if handkerchiefs could have a bad day at the office, was about to have a real stinker. "Just take me a little while to adjust to the heat."

Alberto, who had been first out, was chatting in his native tongue to a man on the ground.

"This is Nolberto, a friend of my father's. He will take us to my village in his boat."

"Very good," said Lee, as he dumped a case in the un-expecting arms of Nolberto.

"Lead the way."

As the boat which could kindly be described as 'having character' bumbled its way downriver, Johnny leant over the side and felt the spray freshen his tired face.

"I wouldn't get too close," Alberto said in a warning tone. "There could be piranha in there."

Although Johnny felt destiny wouldn't bring him all this way just to present him as a starter to some pointy-toothed fish, he pulled away from the edge, better safe than digested. Lee, meanwhile, had the look of a man who knew the other people around him had all come to a common realisation that if the boat was scuppered then they'd at least have a bit of a chance of getting away whilst the fish went to work on him.

Johnny had to admit as he kept his distance from the edge, that the scenery was quite inspiring. The water's edge was lined with lush tree life, and the hoots and howls of local wildlife waltzed through the air. He started to push words around inside his mind…did he has the start of a new song?

"You okay there, Johnny? You look a bit distant," Lee seemed to speak with some sort of genuine care, although he did not yet know Johnny well enough to realise that 'distant' was usually his default setting.

"I'm good, Lee...I think you might be right about this place. I definitely feel creative already."

"Good to hear. Stick with me, Johnny. You won't go wrong."

Chapter Six

"The day is near, son. Finally, the prophecy will be fulfilled. The outsider is near. The Paper Monkey will be with us soon, and our enemies to the east shall suffer for their centuries of ignorance. All this I do for you. Do you understand?"

Being only seven years old, Mateo didn't really have any significant opinion on his father's words, but he knew that if he was quiet and listened than it would soon be playtime and that was all that concerned him at that moment.

"Father, will there be other children for me to play with when we rule the East?"

Basilio smiled at his son's youthful indifference.

"You will be able to do anything you wish."

The tender moment, albeit played out amongst the backdrop of planned murder was interrupted by the entrance of Egecatl, crooked of back and nose, he was the poster boy for wise village elders everywhere.

"I need to speak with you, Basilio. I have…mixed news of the foreigner."

Mateo eyed the old man with suspicion. He had the uncanny knack of spoiling playtime, and now Mateo realised he had listened quietly for no reason.

Basilio saw the look of disappointment in his son's eyes, but could not ignore any warning from the village elder.

"Go play outside for a moment son. I will join you shortly."

Mateo sulked out, making sure to stick his tongue out behind Egecatl's back with as much force as he could muster.

"This had better be important, old man. You know I do not appreciate my time with the boy being interrupted."

"My apologies. But this cannot wait. He is near."

"Then that is excellent news!"

"I'm afraid there is a complication. I have heard that someone else is with them. A boy from the East. He has the tattoo."

"How is that possible? We have not been paying that fat oaf for all these years so that he can hand the Paper Monkey over to one of our enemies!"

Basilio felt his anger rising. They had not come this close to have it all snatched away.

"Egecatl, who else knows about this?"

"Only my spies. They can be trusted."

"Let us hope so. No-one else can know till we have him."

"I understand, Basilio. But…there is something that troubles me. If a son of the East has found him, what if our prophecies are wrong?"

"Do not think of such things. We are right. I know it, deep down. We must move quickly. They must not be allowed to reach the East!"

Mateo kicked a battered football around in frustration as he eagerly eyed the doorway for any sign of his father.

"Can I play, Mateo?"

Mateo despaired, as much as it possible for a seven-year-old to do so anyway.

The questioning voice belonged to Adelfo, his classmate. Standing there in her pigtails, thinking that she could play.

"Girls can't play football. Besides, I'm waiting for my father."

"We can too! I don't see him anywhere."

"He's in the house with Egecatl."

"Stupid smelly old crow-face?"

Mateo couldn't believe that Adelfo would say that out loud. She was clearly mad. Was she trying to get them both turned into lizards?

"Sshhh! You know he can hear through walls."

"Oh don't be silly. My mother says those are just silly stories for silly boys."

Mateo considered this for a second. He certainly didn't want to be turned into a lizard, yet he didn't want to be known as believing in silly tales either.

"If I let you play football with me will you promise to be quiet?"

Adelfo grabbed the ball and kicked it into the air.

"I suppose so."

Mateo watched her run after the ball, and really, really hoped that when he was in the East then there would be no girls allowed.

Thousands of feet up in the air, Baz fidgeted in his seat, poking at his in-flight meal. He had hoped a thirteen-hour flight might provide bigger portions of the colourless lumps that he was moving around with his plastic fork.

"Becky must really love you." Said Laura.

Of course, he knew he was lucky. There weren't many women he knew who would allow their other half to fly thousands of miles with a young girl they had not long met, all in a quest to protect a dopey friend from some old prophecy and mostly himself. Yep, Baz reminded himself as he brought the fork to eye level, examining what was supposed to be chicken chasseur in closer detail. He was a lucky man.

"If she really loved me," said Baz as he braved another mouthful, "she'd have made me stay at home."

Laura laughed, trying not to sound too nervous. She had motored through the last few days so fast that she hadn't really allowed herself to wonder just what the hell she was doing. It was bad enough she had lied to her parents that it was a university-organised trip, although convincing them that going to South America would be of educational merit to a psychology student had been a little trickier. Babbling about the effect on climate and location on the human psyche seemed to have satisfied them. For now, anyway. It wasn't as if she could have told them the truth, was it? Especially as she wasn't sure what the truth was.

"I don't think the clouds are going to talk back," Baz spoke as he saw Laura gazing out of the window, muttering gently to herself.

"That's just something I do when I'm nervous."

"Don't worry about it, I'm a bit nervous myself."

"Really?"

"Yea. I've never been one for travelling really, I mean, you don't get a stamp on your passport for going to Benidorm do you?"

"Not really, no."

"Well, at least I should come back wiser. They do say travel broadens the mind, don't they? I just hope it broadens Johnny's."

Laura noticed the inflexion on Baz's voice as he spoke Johnny's name. There was almost a guilt in there, a regret. She didn't want to push him, but Laura felt that she had to know.

"Baz...why do you feel so responsible for Johnny?"

"It's a long story. You sure you want to hear it?"

Laura smiled. "It can't be any worse than this story that we'll have to tell people one day."

Baz nodded. "That's a good point. Back when I was a student, about fifteen years ago, I was in this band, The Funky Puddles. We used to play a lot of local places, just pub gigs and stuff, but it was a good laugh. I started to notice this skinny little kid hanging around, only about twelve. One day after a gig, he sneaks in the pub, comes up to me and asks if he can audition for the band because he thought our lead singer was rubbish. I mean, to be fair he was right, but we told him where to go. Anyway a few months later, after I'd graduated and the band had broken up, I'm walking down the street and I see these four lads laying into this skinny little kid. I mean, I didn't click at first until I got closer that it was the same kid. They were really giving him a right shoeing, but he kept getting up, I mean in the thirty or so seconds it took me to get to him, he must have been knocked down three or four times, and each time he got up. So anyway I catch up, hand out a few slaps, they scarper, and there's Johnny, dusting off his leather jacket and trying to wipe the blood out of his hair. So I ask him what the fight was about and he says, in this squeaky sort of voice that hadn't broken properly, he says 'they didn't like my t-shirt'. So I look down and he's wearing this faded Funky Puddles t-shirt, that's now all ripped and bloody. I felt so bad for him you know? Still, there was something about the way he kept getting up, he didn't try and run, or call for help. He just kept getting up, because he believed in my silly little student band."

Baz stuttered, his voice cracking slightly as the memory was dusted down and bought to the surface.

"So he's standing there, trying not to cry and I realise that I've got boxes of Funky Puddles t-shirts, CDs and stuff in my mum and dad's garage, so I take him around and he was in heaven. My family sort of unofficially adopted him after that, I suppose. He didn't really have any mates, never knew his old man and his mum isn't exactly what you'd call the maternal type you know?"

Baz fell silent again.

Laura was taken aback. The Johnny she has encountered so far hadn't seemed much more than a two dimensional rock star cartoon with a bad haircut. Horrible as it sounded to admit to herself given the circumstances she was almost relieved to know that there was some reason for the way he was.

"Thanks for telling me that."

Baz regained his composure. "Thanks for not laughing at the thought of me running down the street."

He looked at his watch, there were still six or so hours until they were due to land. "You know if you're in the mood for stories…I've got quite a few more."

So, for the next few hours, Laura was indulged with the not-quite rock n roll history of Paper Monkey. Baz talked about how they were once chased from a village fête by a flock of sheep riled by a heavy bass line, and how an online music magazine once described Johnny as the 'anti-god of rock and roll'. Johnny, being Johnny had taken this as a compliment.

Sometime between hearing about when the band attempted a guerrilla gig on the Blackpool Tower to the inspiration behind 'Harold had a metro', Laura drifted off to sleep.

As she slept, she dreamt in surreal shapes of old legends and ancient gods. She saw crooked figures huddled over boiling pots, chanting words long thought lost. When she woke, she put it down to the recycled plane air, trying to ignore the niggling notion of some divine guiding hand poking its fingers around in her subconscious.

After finding their feet back on solid ground, Alberto found a second whilst Lee had disappeared to relieve himself to approach Johnny about something that had been bothering him.

"Do you actually know where Lee plans to take you?"

"Er, not really. I was just going to wing it. Why change the habit of a lifetime?"

"Well, I think it may be best if you came to my village. Safer." Alberto began to speak in a hushed voice.

"Safer than what?"

"I can't really explain very well, but I'm not sure Lee is…what's the word?"

"Suited to this climate? Tell me about it. I got a feeling his deodorant is really earning its money, you know?"

"No, that's not what I meant, I mean…trustworthy. I'm not sure he's trustworthy."

Johnny took the suggestion with typical ambivalence.

"Well, even if he isn't, Al, it doesn't really matter. I don't need to trust him. I trust destiny."

Alberto wasn't sure he could give Johnny the correct advice, even if they had always spoken the same language. Alberto wanted to tell Johnny that destiny was a fickle thing, that whilst Johnny believed destiny was guiding him toward musical glory, it was quite possible that someone else with the same faith would contradict Johnny's path.

The thing was, Alberto hadn't trusted Lee since the moment he had met him. There was something about him that didn't feel right, snatches of the stories he'd heard as a child seemed to surface whenever he saw the fat man speak to Johnny. Alberto now felt the odd burden that any of Johnny's friends felt. Although he knew that he should leave Johnny to look after himself, he just couldn't bring himself to do it, but how was he going to convince him? It was then, remembering how they had met in the first place that Alberto stumbled upon the correct button to push.

"I'm sure the people in my village would love to hear some of your music."

Johnny, looking delighted at the news suddenly realised that their little posse was a heavy man light.

"I should really wait for Lee. I mean, he did bring me here. I bet he'd like to see your village as well."

Alberto knew what he was about to do might be dishonest, but he didn't see much of an alternative.

"Oh, well, my father should be here to pick us up soon, and Lee told me he was going for a walk, explore the local areas. I gave him directions, he will meet us later."

Alberto watched the eyebrows on Johnny twitch slightly as he processed the given explanation.

"Fair enough."

Emptying his bladder whilst keeping a cautious eye out for the local wildlife, Lee considered his next move. He had done what had been asked of him, so what now? It had been a while since he had received any contact from his mysterious benefactors, and he was starting to get nervous. At what could have been a very dangerous moment had his zip control been of shoddy standard, a voice whispered to him from behind.

"Pssst! Englishman!"

Slowly turning around, Lee couldn't make out the owner of the whisper.

"Up here."

Perched about ten foot above his head in a tree, was a man in his early twenties. His bare feet dangled off the branch, as though his toes were preparing to bungee jump.

"Um, hello. Can I help you?"

"My name is Rudolpho. I was sent to find you and the Paper Monkey, and take you back with me."

"Ah right. And what happens then?"

"Then we have the ritual."

Well, thought Lee. *That didn't sound too bad. Ritual. Good, be a nice occasion, bit of a shindig.*

"The boy from the East cannot come, though. You two must come alone."

The man then slid down from the tree, pointing frantically forward and cursing in a language Lee could not understand.

Turning around once again, Lee could make out what appeared to be Johnny and Alberto climbing onto the back of a truck. Frantically bowling forward through the bush and waving his hands, before he could so much as cry out 'They're leaving without me!' the truck trundled out of view, most definitely leaving without him.

Johnny, peeking behind him as they went down the road caught a glimpse of Lee.

"That's nice. He's waving us off."

Chapter Seven

Mateo was not a happy boy. Not only had his father not come out to play, but more men had started to arrive. One of them was a very big, very pale man that Mateo did not recognise. To make things worse, not only was Adelfo much better at football than him but she actually seemed to realise it. In all his seven years, this day was turning out to be one of the worst.

Inside the house, Basilio was having a similarly bad day, albeit for different reasons than his son.

"What do you mean he got away?"

Rudolpho squirmed and looked at Egecatl for assistance that was not forthcoming.

"I found the man like you asked, and then…the boy from the East took the Paper Monkey away in a truck. I couldn't do anything."

Basilio turned away, fixing his angry stare at the wall.

"Get out of my sight. Tell him to wait, I will send for him."

"Do not be too hard on Rudolpho. He is still young, he tried his best," Egecatl reasoned.

"Well, his best is not enough, and I can't help but wonder about your judgement old man."

Egecatl shifted his weight and straightened his back, suddenly seeming far less old and fragile.

"I would remind you, Basilio, that I was trying to fulfil the prophecy when you were still suckling at you mothers teat like a piglet. It would serve you best not to question my judgement."

Basilio put his anger in check. It was best to keep the old man on his side, for now anyway.

"My apologies. In my anger, I forgot myself."

"It is okay. These are stressful times," replied Egecatl, reverting to his normal posture.

Had Lee heard the wise old man's wise old words, he might have been inclined to agree. Standing nervously outside a house in a strange place in a strange country, he wondered just what the hell he was doing here. It was if someone had clicked their fingers and he had been bought out of hypnosis. Had he really travelled to Peru on the advice of some far-away voice on the telephone? The damn heat wasn't helping any. He couldn't tell what sweat was nerves and what sweat was down to the temperature. Not aiding his anxious state was the fixed stares of a young boy and girl a few feet away from him. Beginning to wonder whether he should have taken his chances with the piranha, the young duo edged their way slowly towards him, chattering quietly to each other in what sounded like the same language as Rudolpho, though he couldn't be sure.

As they were just a few feet away, the door behind him swung open and a wizened hand beckoned him inside. Weighing the merits of rock against those of a hard place, Lee cautiously made his way in.

"Who do you think that was, Mateo?"

"I don't know. Probably something to do with the prophecy, I suppose."

Adelfo sniffed at the suggestion. "My mother says the prophecy is just silly stories for silly boys."

Mateo, offended without understanding why, felt the need to defend his family's honour. Was there anything her mother didn't think was a silly story for silly boys?

"My father is not a silly boy. He's a man, and your mother will change her mind when we rule the East."

"Well, I don't understand why he wants to go there anyway."

"Because it's in the prophecy. Everyone knows that."

"Yes but why? He has the biggest house in the village here."

Mateo despaired. *Why did she have to ask so many questions?*

"Because, that's why. And if you ever want to play with my ball again you better stop asking about it!"

Adelfo, falling mercifully silent and filling Mateo with a false hope that she might stay that way, tilted her head toward the sky as though in deep thought, before asking

"Why?"

It was a question that Basilio was repeating to himself inside. Why had they wasted his village's fortune on this stranger? Why had he entrusted young fools to bring the Paper Monkey to him? All questions that would have to wait, a false face of friendly intent would have to serve him for now.

"It is a pleasure to finally meet you. You have served us well."

Lee shook a hand that gripped like a vice with a vendetta. It didn't *feel* like a pleasure.

"Well, the pleasure is all mine. It's nice to put a face to the voice," Lee had been in the music industry long enough to know when someone was lying, and when to lie back.

"The voice you've heard hasn't been mine."

This prompted Egecatl to emerge from the shadows, beak first. Taking a step back, Lee very much wished he hadn't had the opportunity to match a voice to that particular face.

"My name is Egecatl, the village elder. When I first made contact, Basilio here was barely a man. I have been teaching him English, in anticipation of our meeting."

"Well, you both speak it very well. Could I er, ask just how you speak it so well?"

"My father was a well-travelled man, he saw much of the world. He said the man who speaks in many tongues may whisper charms in many ears."

Lee cringed and wondered if Egecatl's father had spent time opening Chinese crackers on his travels.

"He sounds like a wise man."

Egecatl chuckled in a disturbing way as Lee had ever heard, like a vulture choking down a kitten.

"Well, it was he who discovered you. He heard your…'music' and believed you would play an important role in fulfilling our prophecies."

This perked up Lee more than it had any right to, especially given the inflexion on 'music'. The mere fact this man's father had heard his music made him feel much more at ease. In fact, he felt more than at ease, suddenly feeling as though his own destiny was finally making sense. Had it led him here to show him how far his music had travelled? That it had touched people with a purpose far greater than he could have ever imagined?

"I don't suppose he's still around, is he? I would like to meet him." Lee said, eager to impress a fan for the first time.

"His body passed on years ago. But his spirit is here with us in this room. He is very pleased you have made it this far."

"Ah right, of course," Lee looked around the room, ducking slightly just in case the friendly apparition was floating over his head. "Well…tell him he's very welcome."

Camping outside the doorway, Mateo and Adelfo were involved in a good old-fashioned game of chicken.

"You should go in. You do live there."

"I know I live there, but I'm not supposed to go in when the adults are doing…whatever it is they do."

"If you ask me…you're scared, Mateo. If I lived there, I'd go in."

Not for the first time that afternoon, Mateo felt his not fully developed male ego pricked, and he didn't like it.

"Well, my father says I should never listen to a girl."

"You listen to your mother don't you?"

"That's different, everyone listens to their mother."

Finally, silence. He had done it. Mateo savoured the victory. Any self-satisfaction was soon interrupted, by the unsettling sound of a wobbly lip.

"You're mean, Mateo! And smelly!"

With that last remark, she ran off, leaving Mateo with a mixed sense of relief and shame. Not about being smelly, he was sure he'd been tricked into a bath at some point in the last few days. Whilst relieved she was gone, he also felt bad about it, although once again it was a feeling he couldn't wrap his seven-year-old brain around.

"Mateo!"

His father's booming voice cut through the air.

"I'm afraid I have no time to play, son. Go and play with your friends. I'm sure Adelfo will be happy to play. I think she likes you."

Watching his father march back into the house, Mateo was left feeling both disappointed and confused. When this Paper Monkey showed up, he was going to have some very nasty faces to pull behind its back.

"Are you sure this is a live music venue?" Johnny asked the question as he looked around the bar in Alberto's village. Hardly in a position to be picky about his live venues, Johnny had to admit to himself that it did have some sort of rustic charm. After all, there was a couple of old drunks finely balanced on rickety schools, and a one-eyed barman who made Buster Head look welcoming, behind whom a flickering neon sign illumed the words 'Al's Bar'.

"Of course." Said Alberto. " My father owns it."

"Al, your old man owns a bar and now you tell me?"

Alberto shrugged. "It didn't come up."

"Even worse, your old man owns a bar and you don't like drinking?"

Alberto motioned toward the drunks on stools. "That is exactly why."

Johnny, viewing the sign again and having that all too rare light bulb of his own going off, realised something else.

"And that would be why you don't like being called Al."

"Ah, the wisdom of the Paper Monkey."

"Al, did you just make a joke?"

Alberto shrugged. "Well, maybe I did learn something on my travels after all."

Later, as Johnny strummed his guitar, warbling his lyrics to the already merry locals, Alberto took the opportunity to seek council from the village elders. As much as he had always tried to maintain a cynicism when it came to prophecy and myth, the events of the last few days couldn't be ignored. Plus, Alberto had never been as nervous as other people when it came to talking to the elders, in fact, he had never had much choice in the matter. Alberto pushed open the door to the modest house, and sure enough, there was the old man sitting in his favourite chair, wrinkled brow deep in thought.

"Hello, Grandfather."

"Well, well. The traveller returns. So, do you come back wiser?"

"I don't know about that. I've learnt a few things though."

"Hmm. Come sit by me, boy, let me look at you."

Alberto duly obliged, dragging a stool in front of the old man. Behind them, a fire crackled with life. Alberto had never seen the house without a fire, whatever the weather. His grandfather, Alvarez, claimed it was so he could 'keep an eye on the spirits'.

Alvarez placed his right hand on Alberto's forehead, as though he were checking his temperature and muttered something ancient that even Alberto couldn't have translated.

"Grandfather?" Alberto had been used to the ancient muttering but the hand on the head thing was new.

"Ssssh, boy. Just looking around in there. Hmm. So there's a woman involved."

"What? No, not really. I mean, I had to leave her behind. It wasn't as though I could bring her here…even if I had wanted to."

The old man roared a throaty "Ha!" at this. "Perhaps she isn't as left behind as you think."

In his tired, jet-lagged state, Alberto didn't try and make sense of his grandfather's cryptic musings.

"Don't you want to know where he is?"

"I already know where he is. Not that your father's bar seems a fitting place for the Paper Monkey spirit," the Old man paused for a second before the irony of the spirit surrounded by spirits of a different kind occurred to him. "Then again, I suppose he's as safe there as anywhere. Still, we must be careful. If the West has your other friend, then they will come looking for the Paper Monkey."

"I wouldn't really call him a friend, Grandfather."

"Hmm, from what I see in the flames I would say that is a wise choice. He was corrupted long ago, without even realising it."

"Corrupted how?"

"The elders of the West found him, manipulated him. They gave him all their gold, trying to find the Paper Monkey. There's nothing wrong with dreaming, boy. But there are some men who would use a man's dreams to destroy him."

"You saw all this in the flames?"

"The two eyes I have in my head aren't the only ones I see through."

Alberto tried to listen in-between the words. A realisation was starting to form, and it was one he didn't like.

"Grandfather, when you sent me to England, did you know?"

Alvarez gave a nonchalant shrug of his wise old shoulders. "As much as I know anything. But enough of that. Tell me more about this girl. And don't you dare pretend you don't know what I'm talking about."

At roughly that moment and at least now finally in the same country, Laura was trying to ignore the strange burning sensation in her ears.

She stared at the map in her hands, as though doing so might conjure some magical marker pointing to their location. It had been a good few hours since a chuckling taxi driver had taken them 'as far south as he could' and Laura was starting to doubt the accuracy of those travel websites.

"Are you sure this is the right way?" Baz wrestled with the straps on his backpack before relieving himself of the weight by letting it drop to the floor.

"I'd know for certain if only my so-called smart-phone would get a signal," she waved the device in the air, in the time-honoured fashion of those desperate for a few bars.

"Well, I vote for a breather," Baz fought for his breath as he joined his backpack on the floor.

Laura too flopped to the ground, throwing the map with as much force as paper can be thrown, it fluttered lightly to the floor, as if to mock her effort.

"I'm sorry, Baz. God, I've dragged you halfway around the world and I'm not even sure why, and now we're stuck in the middle of nowhere."

Baz shuffled over to her on his backside like a dog with worms and put a friendly arm around her shoulder.

"Everywhere is somewhere, and I chose to come. A wise man once said, 'long is the road, beware the vengeful toad'."

Laura looked at Baz and could only guess that the humidity and jet lag were getting to him. Then it dawned on her. "Was that one of your lyrics?"

"Yea," replied Baz. "We were pretty shit to be honest. Definitely not worth getting beat up over."

"So what now?" Laura asked after she had allowed herself to laugh a little. "What do we do when we actually find them?"

"Well," replied Baz. "If Johnny hasn't already been chased out of the village by an angry mob, then I'll try and talk some sense into him."

"Will that work?"

Baz laughed at the question.

"There's a first time for everything."

They both took to staring at the horizon, deep in thought. It was then that Baz spotted something that he hoped wasn't some sort of motoring mirage.

"Laura, stick your thumb out."

"Why?"

"Because who would you stop for, a young woman in need, or a sweaty fat bald bloke with a sunburnt head?"

Laura stepped to the side of the road and, realising that perhaps now was not the time for a lecture on exploitation, jacked her thumb into the air. "Point taken. But I am not fluttering my bloody eyelashes."

Eventually, a truck pulled up, and a young man lent out of the window, seemingly proving Baz's point.

Laura, with a little visual encouragement from Baz, walked up to the cab window, the map still clutched in hand.

"Excuse me, do you speak English?"

"A little. You need help?"

Laura pointed at a spot on the map, which if the driver's eyebrows were anything to go by, he seemed to recognise.

"You are a long way away."

"Could you take us?" Laura asked earnestly. "We think our friend could be headed that way and lost."

"It's your lucky day," said the driver. "I'm going that way. Get in."

Laura and Baz climbed into the truck behind the good Samaritan, who seemed very eager to have them.

Baz shook his hand. "I'm Baz, this is Laura. You're a lifesaver mate."

"No problem. My name is Rudolpho."

Chapter Eight

"So what did you think?"

Johnny optimistically awaited an answer from the locals at Al's.

"They don't speak English. Most of the time they don't speak much of anything."

The mystery answer was soon followed by a man who emerged from a side door at the end of the bar. Nodding to the barman, he soon had a shot placed in front of him.

"I'm Al."

Shaking his hand, Johnny could see the resemblance between Al senior and junior. One very striking resemblance, seeing as Al was sporting a vest.

"I see you have the tattoo."

"Of course, but that's nothing special. Half the men here do. Not all of them made it out into the big wide world though." Al said before downing the shot.

"So you went travelling as well, where did they send you?" Johnny asked.

"To England, like my son. How do you think he speaks it so well?"

"I thought he was a fast learner. Seems pretty bright."

"I've always thought so." Replied Al with more than a hint of pride. "And now he brings us you, the Paper Monkey."

"Well, I don't know about that." Said Johnny. "I just had these dreams, and then I saw the tattoo and…well, I've always believed in destiny. Not quite sure how my destiny adds up with your Paper Monkey but…I suppose I'm along for the ride."

Al motioned to his barman for another drink with one hand, whilst making another motion with his other hand toward the bar-hogging locals that they seemed to understand as home time, they all headed for the door, shuffling, moaning and groaning like extras from a zombie film.

"My son tells me you were bought here by another man, some record producer. How well do you know this man?" Al gestured Johnny toward one of the now vacant bar stools.

"About as well as I know anyone else here, but he did give us a contract. Well, me. I was in a band until a few days ago. Till they…'till I ditched them. I don't think they could have handled it here anyway, it's all too big for them," Johnny tried his best to sound like he wasn't missing them, it wasn't working well.

"Johnny, how much do you know about our village, it's history?" Al asked as he slid a drink toward Johnny along the bar with an impressive speed and lack of spill.

"Just that you all worship some monkey god or something." Replied Johnny. "Funny that I should call my band the same thing eh? Well, unless it is destiny and all that,"

"The people here, we are more how can I say, relaxed about such things. We follow our traditions, we respect them, but they do not rule us. Not the same can be said for everyone. To the west is a village with similar beliefs, but they are far more serious about things than us. Do you understand what I'm telling you, Johnny?"

Johnny didn't understand. He wasn't expecting a geography lesson or a history one for that matter. He started to wonder whether separating from Lee had been such a good idea.

"Not really. Don't worry though. Once my manager catches up with us, everything will be sorted. I think he's got a plan."

"It's not his plans that concern me. I think to be safe you should stay with us tonight."

"Sound. That's very nice of you," Johnny was certainly not about to turn down a free bed at a bar.

"Good, it will keep my father off my back as well. You would not believe the trouble it causes being the son of the village elder."

"Does he not drink either?"

"Oh, he drinks plenty," said Al, a wince in his voice. "He just doesn't pay for it."

Inside his grandfather's home, Alberto filled by his grandmother's cooking and drained by his grandfather's questioning, sat back and stared at the flames once more.

"When does it start making sense?"

"What, boy, the fire?"

"Life."

Alvarez let out a gentler, more wistful laugh than the belly laughs of which he had previously.

"Doesn't matter how far you travel, or how wise you become. It never will. Why do you think people put such faith in prophecies? In religion? It gives people a grounding, something to believe in when times are hard."

Alberto looked at his grandfather in admiration. Sometimes he was reminded just why the old man was the chief village elder.

"Do you believe that Johnny is the Paper Monkey?" Alberto asked.

Alvarez chuckled once more, eighty plus years of wisdom condensing his face into a quizzical smile.

"I'm open to the suggestion."

Laura kept one eye on the map and one eye on the road as Rudolpho's truck rattled along. They had been travelling for hours, and she had long lost any sense of where they were. Suddenly pulling up, their driver paused for a second, in the manner of a man searching his mind for the correct translation.

"Excuse me. I have to, er…" He looked at Baz and pointed loosely at his own crotch.

Baz, seemingly understanding via some unseen bladder related male bond, nodded in recognition.

Laura waited until Rudolpho was out of the cab and out of hearing range before she spoke.

"I'm not sure about this Baz. I'm trying to follow on the map, but I can't tell where he's taking us."

"Well, he's a local, probably knows all the short cuts. I wouldn't worry too much. Besides, I really am not in the mood for more walking."

Laura rubbed her own aching legs. "Me either. Still, if he tries anything funny…"

"Well, when he gets back in I'll have a little word," Baz said reassuringly.

A few moments later, when Rudolpho had got back behind the wheel, Baz tried his best to be nonchalant.

"Are we close mate?"

Rudolpho gave a little nod of his own and grinned.

"Nearly there."

Alberto had stopped by the bar on the way home, to find Johnny and his father engaged in some good old-fashioned whiskey-based male bonding.

"Ah, my son! Fulfiller of the prophecy! You know for a skinny man, this Paper Monkey you brought home can handle his drink."

Alberto sighed and said something to Al senior that Johnny couldn't understand.

Whatever it was, Al disagreed with it.

"Well, you can tell your grandfather he can settle his tab before he starts talking about anything else. Sitting there, staring at those damned flames…"

"Your old man has got some great stories. Did you know that he once went out with -"

"I've heard the stories," said Alberto, cutting Johnny off and staring daggers at his father, who was swaying with a happy grin on his face.

"Johnny, do you mind if I have a word with 'my old man' in private please?"

Even in his inebriated state, Johnny knew when a family domestic was about to take place, and decided to go and get some fresh air. After all, if he wanted to see a son row with his parents he would have just stayed at home and done it himself.

Waiting for Johnny to leave the room, Alberto reverted back to his natural tongue.

"What are you doing, Dad?"

Al senior looked over both shoulders to see if anyone had sneaked-up on him because he knew his son surely wasn't asking him that question.

"What, you think you're all grown up now because you've been away for a few months? You think you can come in here and question me? I'm still your father, Alberto, doesn't matter how many prophecies you've fulfilled!"

"I...this isn't about prophecies. I left Johnny here because I thought you'd be responsible, not get him drunk!"

Alberto felt panic set in. He'd never spoken like this to his father before. This was unknown territory, and he had no idea where he was going to end up. And now...now there was a look in his father's eyes that Alberto didn't want to see. A look that said '*My little boy, who used to think of me as a great hero, now has no respect for me. My little boy who thinks he's a man and doesn't need me anymore*'.

Al turned his back and drained the last of a bottle into his glass, before turning back and raising it in a mock toast.

"Well, good luck to you, son, now that you're a big responsible man of the world."

Alberto muttered a curse under his breath to whatever Gods, local or not, might be listening. If the prophecy was going to come between him and his father than he wanted no part of it. After all, if the Paper Monkey was so wonderful why would it come between fathers and sons, why would it turn brothers and neighbours into enemies? Why would it...

As these thoughts and more crashed upon the shore of his mind, Alberto suddenly realised something.

"Where's Johnny?"

The warm night breeze ruffled Johnny's abundant bouffant and massaged his troubled mind. Why was he here again? The whiskey whispered at his brain, told him not to worry about such things and find whatever passed for a late-night fast food take away in these parts. Still, there was that rare part of him, that all too often ignored the voice of common sense that poked at him from somewhere deep inside. Very, very deep, in Johnny's case.

He had come all this way, left his band and best…only friends behind. He glanced upward at the night sky, as clear as he had ever seen. Stars twinkled like little forget-me-nots, promises of light from galaxies far, far away. *Maybe that's my problem,* he thought. *I've been on a different planet my whole life. Too much looking up and not enough looking around…*

A footstep to his side snapped Johnny into a state of alertness that came from years of avoiding gig-goers asking for their money back.

An old man, wearing what looked in the moonlight like a tattered cape and resting his weight on a gnarled wooden cane stood before him.

"Johnny, I presume?"

"Does everyone in this village speak perfect English?"

The old man gave a smile so warm Johnny could have wrapped himself up and gone to sleep in it.

"Only those of us that need to. May I ask why you are wandering alone at night, in a place where you have no idea where you are?"

"Well, I was over at Al's bar, but then I got the feeling the two of them, I mean, the two Al's that is were about to have a bit of a row…so I came out for some air."

"The two of them? Which two do you mean?"

"Young Al and his old man, Al senior. You know them?"

The old man's features changed somewhat. He suddenly looked far less friendly, and the cane suddenly looked far more solid.

"That would be my son and grandson, both of whom are supposed to be watching you."

"Oh. I haven't got them into trouble, have I?"

The smile returned to the old man's face. "Not yet."

'The two Als' as they had now been christened by Johnny, scrambled out of the bar, both secretly grateful for the interruption to their first real Father-Son barney in a while.

"Which way do you think he went?" Al junior turned to his father, quickly regressing and hoping his dad, who he was just shouting at, would know how to sort this all out.

Al senior looked into the night, the fear of his father's judgement was very quickly burning up the alcohol in his system.

"How should I know? He's a grown man he—"

The two Al's spied two figures approaching through the darkness and waited for them to come into the light.

Al seniors' heart sank. The old man had found him, of course, he had found him. What else had he expected?

Alvarez arrived in front of his offspring, slowly shaking his head in the way parents do as if to give a warning shot to their children that a biblical bollocking is shortly to follow.

"I should have known better," he said, "than to leave poor Johnny here with you. He is our guest and an important one at that. Would you like to explain to me why he is wandering around the village on his own at night, and drunk at that?"

Al senior looked down sheepishly, feeling forty years younger. "I was just trying to make him feel welcome. If you hadn't kept Alberto so late…"

Johnny, feeling slightly guilty for coming between the Pablez men, decided to play peacemaker.

"It's my fault, I should have said where I was going. No harm done, eh?"

Alvarez nodded. "Perhaps the wisdom of the Paper Monkey is in you yet. Alberto, take Johnny home and put him to bed. Tomorrow, Johnny, you will come to my home and we will talk. As for you, my son, I should speak with you in private."

Alberto duly departed, keeping an eye on Johnny. There was no way he was getting on his grandfather's wrong side.

Now alone outside the bar, Alvarez turned to Al.

"So what do you think?"

"You know my thoughts on the prophecy."

Alvarez sighed. "That is not what I meant. Do you not feel as though you have seen Johnny somewhere before?"

"I don't know," shrugged Al. "I suppose he looks familiar now that you mention it. I couldn't say where from though."

"A face from the past, I'm sure of it. Perhaps when you are sober, it will come to you. Now, back to the bar."

"You're not serious?"

The old man raised his cane and pointed it under his son's nose. "You've had plenty to drink. I, however, still need my nightcap."

Laura jumped awake. The heat and the travel squashed against her memories. Where the hell was she? Then slowly but surely, recognition cranked through the gears and she knew. She was still in the truck, with a still sleeping Baz, and their mysterious driver was nowhere to be seen. A glance through the truck's window at least told her she was in a populated area, the truck was parked in front of a comfortably large house.

"Baz!"

Cautiously, she poked at the big man between his ribs, which whilst conjuring a childish giggle that belied his frame, did little else.

"Baz, wake up!" She found herself shouting in a whisper, and then wondered how that was even possible.

Baz stirred, as though he were some great mythical beast that had lay in hibernation for decades, and then for good measure made a noise like one.

"Wrrrrffgggghhh?"

"Baz, you need to…" Laura considered her options. What would puncture his comatose consciousness? "Baz, it's dinner time!"

That did it. Baz shot up, and Laura would later swear the whole truck did like-wise.

Blinking in the dim light, his mind went through the same unfolding of memories that Laura's had done moments before.

"There's no dinner, is there?" Baz spoke as though he had accepted the fact, though the tiniest portion of hope carried in his tone.

"I'm sorry, Baz, it's the only thing I could think of."

"Are we in the village yet?"

"We're in a village. I just don't think it's Alberto's."

"Well, right village or not, I'm getting out," said Baz. "Nature cal..." he cut himself off as he spied a face leaving the house in front of them, a face he hadn't been too keen on the first time around.

Lee approached the truck nervously, a gun to his head, metaphorically if not literally.

What he didn't realise was that one of the occupants of the said truck was about to come to him.

Baz barrelled out of the truck with a speed that made no sense to Lee. *Nothing that big should be able to move that fast*, he thought, *after all, I should know.*

"Where is he you bloody con-man? Where's Johnny?"

Baz had Lee by the sweat-encrusted lapels.

"He's er, well, I don't quite know to be honest. Last time I saw him he was disappearing into the distance with that Alberto lad, and my luggage at that."

"You left him alone?"

"Actually he left me alone, in the middle of nowhere." Lee stammered in indignation. "You know, I get the impression that Alberto lad doesn't trust me."

"I wonder why! And how did you turn up here then?"

"The same way you did by the look of it."

Baz released Lee from his grip and noticed Rudolpho standing nonchalantly in the doorway.

Laura, who had now caught up, decided she was not in the mood to be polite. After all, by the look of things, they had been kidnapped. Sort of.

"Am I the only one who wants to know just where the fuck 'here' is?"

"I'm still not entirely sure on the where, but I can fill you in on some of the why," said Lee. "The big chief in there, well without going into too much detail, it appears that he's been sort of funding me all these years. Anyway, turns out they were looking for their Paper Monkey, and they thought it might turn out to be a musician, and what with everything that's happened with Johnny and the symbol…"

"We know all about the symbol and the beliefs and all that other bollocks, Laura found it all in a book," Baz was eyeing Lee like a Rottweiler might eye a cat that had had the temerity to venture into its back garden.

"You're telling me…that when you invited us down to London you knew about all this?"

"No, no!" Lee could feel the eyes in the back of his head coming from the direction of the house. They were surely going to see that this was not going well.

"It wasn't like that, not at all. They…they got in my head somehow, it was all very confusing, like living in a dream, or a nightmare…"

Basilio eyed the action from inside the house. The pretender had seemingly exaggerated his friendship with the two new strangers.

"Where did you say Rudolpho found these two?"

Egecatl emerged from the shadows, which seemed to follow him no matter where he stood in a room.

"Lost, in the North. They were trying to get to the East, there must be a connection. The fates sent them here, I'm certain of it. If they know the Paper Monkey, they can be used as…leverage to bring him here more easily."

Basilio didn't take his eyes away from the scene outside.

"Then it appears you were right about Rudolpho. He has done well. For once."

"Indeed," Egecatl tried not to sound too smug. "May I suggest a little diplomatic intervention by the head of the village?"

"I suppose. But I warn you, diplomacy is starting to bore me."

Basilio strode out of the house, extending his arms and wearing a false smile that the most committed of holiday reps would have been proud of.

"Welcome! Welcome!" He grabbed Baz by the hand and gave it a hearty shake.

Laura, noticing that Baz had been thrown off his stride by the sudden appearance of the man wearing what looked like some sort of ceremonial robe, stepped in front of him.

"Welcome to where exactly? He…" she pointed with a glare at Rudolpho, still languishing in the doorway, "…said he would take us here!" she thrust the map in front of Basilio's face.

Gently taking the map out of Laura's hands, Basilio studied where she was pointing.

"I see. Let me speak to him," beckoning Rudolpho over with a motion of his hand, Basilio lent in as Rudolpho whispered something in his ear.

"I see," Basilio turned back to the waiting faces of Laura, Baz and Lee who wasn't quite sure which side he should be standing on.

"My friend here says that the road you need is blocked because of a tree that came down in a storm and that he thought it best to bring you here. He apologises for the misunderstanding, his English is not as strong as mine."

90

"Well, how did—" Lee was cut off by a glance from Basilio that suggested finishing his sentence was not the best of ideas. "Never mind."

"You must be very tired," Basilio looked at Baz. "And hungry. You are welcome to stay here in my village until the road is cleared, and then Rudolpho will take you. Tell me, do you have friends there?"

Baz went to speak then looked at Laura, who hoped that he had understood her most subtle of head shakes.

Producing the book from her bag, Laura found the relevant page.

"We're keen students of world cultures, you know, ancient religions, century-old feuds, gold-filled temples. That sort of thing."

"Then you are in luck, girl," Basilio's friendly facade slipped on the final word. "'That sort of thing' will not need to be found," He leaned forward, towering over Laura, "You might find that those things find you."

Basilio stepped back, putting his friendly face back on.

"Fortunately, we have an empty house on the far side of the village. It's only small, but I'm sure it will do until the road is clear," he turned to Lee. "You stay here."

"This is ridiculous, we're not just going to go to some random house, who the h—"

It was Baz's turn to give Laura a subtle 'don't say anymore' look. He knew that now was not the time and definitely not the place to start arguing.

Chapter Nine

"You," Egecatl had Lee cornered back in the house. "You told me that you were friends with them."

"Yes, well. I was rather hoping that I would be."

"I like to think of myself as a patient man. But I feel that everyone is trying very hard to get in the way of my destiny. Do you understand?"

Lee didn't. He couldn't quite put his finger on what Egecatl was getting at. If it was intimidation, then it was a wasted effort. Not because Lee possessed an iron will, but because he was now so beyond any old concepts of fear that he used to hold before this had happened. Still, a question that he hoped his mouth would ignore somehow wriggled in front of his cowardice.

"Your destiny? Only I was under the impression that it was more of a shared thing."

"Only weak men like you would entertain such ideas. What fool would wish to share power?"

"This, ah, this ritual I've heard mentioned a few times now. Is it due to happen any time soon?"

"The first full moon of the month. Not long, we believe."

"And you need me for it, do you?"

"For now."

Lee felt that strange feeling again. Whatever part Egecatl had lined up for him, Lee was guessing that it wasn't handing out the canapés.

Laura paced the floor of her temporary home. This wasn't right. She had anticipated that things might not go exactly to plan, but this? This she had not accounted for, and she hated that.

"We've had a long journey. You should have a lie-down."

"How can you be so calm, Baz? We've been kidnapped by some...nutter who most likely wants to sacrifice your best mate and you're sitting down?"

"You're assuming that we've been kidnapped and that that bloke is a nutter. You know that these people could be genuinely trying to help us."

"Do you really think so?" Laura wanted to believe Baz. There was something in his gentle tone that almost made her believe him. Almost.

"Well, what about that Lee? What was all that about? You didn't seem so relaxed then!"

"Of course not," said Baz. "He's a record exec."

"A record exec who you know was bringing Johnny to Peru and who just happens to be here? Come on Baz, you know this isn't right!"

"I know that I'm going to get some kip, and you should do the same, alright?"

Not that she wanted to admit it, to herself let alone anyone else, but Laura was exhausted. Pulling a blanket from her pack, she allowed herself to slide to the floor.

"Maybe...maybe I'll just rest my eyes for ten minutes. But then we're getting out of here and we're going to sort this out, deal?"

"You're the boss."

And with that, Laura drifted off.

Al senior sat, stuck in a rut of restlessness. Something his father said yesterday had troubled him, which wasn't all that unusual. What he had said about Johnny bearing a resemblance to someone in his past stuck in his head, scratching away at the forefront of his mind, an answer that he was sure he knew, somewhere deep down. It could be nothing, he had met hundreds of people on his travels, brushed past thousands. Why was this face haunting his memory? He stared at the tattoo on his arm, which usually evoked the widest range of memories. The day he had it done, watching with pride as Alberto had received his...and then another memory, one long-buried under the rubble of his life. It dug its way up, faint at first. The sort of memory so vague at first that it seems only like the edge of a pale watercolour dream, faded in time. Then the image exploded in front of Al's eyes, a firework of remembrance. He could see it all...a night on his travels in England, a fellow lover of spirits, a bet and a seedy tattoo parlour...and a camera? That was it! Al sprang to his feet and sought out the evidence. From the bottom of a trunk, he pulled out his old photo album, leafing through years of celluloid memories until the right one jumped out at him...and there it was.

Himself, depressingly younger, flexing a muscular, tattooed arm and next to him in a mirror pose...the hair was slightly different, and he was a bigger build but the eyes...the eyes were identical. They stared out at him. Al turned over the photo, and there in his youthful scribble was written 'Buster Heads Tattoo parlour, September 25th, 1985. Tommy Rocket gets the tribal ink!'

Al's mind raced. How could he not have realised sooner? This could change everything…

Johnny stared at the flames as he had been instructed, but he didn't feel anything other than warm.

Rosy-cheeked, he turned to Alvarez, throned in his usual seat. "Am I doing this right?"

"There is no right way. If the flames speak, they speak. If not…"

Johnny turned back to the fire, peering intently. "I get the gist."

This was not how he had envisaged spending his creative break. He knew there was something happening that he wasn't being told and whilst this had been a common theme throughout his life it didn't make him any more comfortable with the fact.

As the old man behind him chanted quietly in something indecipherable, Johnny wondered if any of his musical idols had looked into the flames for inspiration. Metaphorically they probably all had, literally some of them had gone up in them. But Johnny knew the likelihood of an amazing melody crackling its way through the air and into his mind was unlikely. Absent-mindedly, he began to tap his fingers on the floor.

tap-tap-taptaptaptap-tap-tap-tap

After a few seconds of this, Alvarez said, "What is that?"

"What's what?"

"That noise. What is that?"

"Noise? Oh, just me tapping on the floor. I don't even know I'm doing it half the time."

"Still nothing from the flames?"

tap-tap-tap-taptap-taptap tap tap tap-tap-tap-tap

"I'm afraid not. Maybe I just don't have the right...whatever for flame watching."

taptaptaptaptap-tap-tap-tap

Alvarez cleared his throat. "Perhaps you do not see anything. But that does not mean you don't feel anything. If you, let's say...didn't even realise you were feeling it."

tap-taptaptaptaptap-tap

"I'm not sure I foll-oooh," recognition struck Johnny late as he looked down at his independently tapping hand.

"You, er, you think this is because of the flames?"

Alvarez gave one of his chuckles. "What do you think?"

"I think," said Johnny. "That I better get my guitar."

When Al senior arrived at his father's house, Johnny was still sitting in front of the fire, now with the guitar across his lap.

"Enjoying the flames, Johnny?" asked Al. He wanted to consult with Alvarez before dropping this on Johnny.

Johnny nodded, trance like with eyes closed as he strummed the guitar to the crackle of the dancing flames.

Alvarez, spotting the urgency in his son's eyes made a polite excuse to Johnny and led him into the kitchen.

"You were right," Al pulled the photo from a pocket. "About something from my past, you were right. This man's name was Tommy Rocket, I had forgotten all about him until..."

Alvarez studied the photo. "The resemblance is uncanny…and you are sure of the name?"

"Yes. He must be Johnny's father!" said Al.

Slightly later, when Alberto had also been summoned to the impromptu kitchen summit, the Pablez men sat around a table on which the photo now took centre stage.

"So, what does this say for the prophecy then?" Al aimed his question at Alvarez.

"The prophecy doesn't change, nor should the way we view it. You talk as if this photo just magicked its way into existence. It did not, it's been sitting in your album for three decades. Besides, I don't remember acknowledging our guitar playing friend in there as the fulfiller of the legacy."

"That's not what you told Alberto!"

"What I told my grandson, is that I was open to the idea, as I am open to all ideas."

"All ideas?" Al spat back. "How about the idea of paying your tab?"

Alvarez swatted away the notion like a troublesome fly. "The village elder has never paid for his own drinks. You know this."

"I know that's what you've always told me!" Al grumbled to himself. He didn't even know why he bought it up, it was never going to happen.

Alberto, who hadn't been able to wrestle his gaze away from the photo since he had sat down, realised he was going to have to step in and break up the paternal argument breaking out.

"It was a memory," he spoke quietly at first, softly to himself as though he were asking his own mind a question.

"Say again, boy?" Alvarez turned one side of his head toward his grandson as though his ear was an aerial that needed constant fiddling with to pick up a signal.

Alberto went on, louder this time as he became more sure of the ideas forming in his head.

"The night when Johnny came and introduced himself to me, he...he had all these scraps of paper with the drawing of the tattoo. He said it had come to him in a dream but what if it wasn't a dream? What if it was a memory?"

"Makes sense to me. There's no destiny at work here, just coincidence," Al senior spoke as though the case was solved in his mind.

Alvarez retorted with a derisory snort. "And what is 'coincidence'? Is it not just a word for those that do not believe in a higher power? A guiding hand? You, my son, were sent out into the world. You meet a total stranger, he copies your tattoo, and years later his son meets yours and you think that is a coincidence?"

"Well, like you just said father, it's a word for people who don't believe."

Al's sentence brought a hush that settled upon the room like an ancient curse.

"I'm not asking you to believe, my son," said Alvarez. "All I've ever asked is that you be open to believing."

Johnny was just about aware of the raised voices coming from the other room, but it was like being aware of thunder from a distant storm. Eyes still fixed on the flames, he felt melodies and words float in his head. Chords danced and weaved together in his mind's eye. It came as quite a shock to Johnny, in his state of creative bliss, when something hit him hard on the back of the head and he blacked out.

"What you don't seem to be mentioning old man, is what happens if that bastard Basilio finds out about this. You know how extreme those people are about the prophecy. The safest thing for Johnny is if we get him on the first plane back to England!"

A noise from the other room punctured the arguing. Al senior reacted first, dashing out to find the guitar lying without its owner. Without so much as a 'told you so' to Alvarez, he yelled at Alberto to follow and ran out of the door.

Half an hour or so later, a now breathless Al and son returned to the house of Alvarez, to find the old man now back in his chair.

"We can't find him anywhere…and no-one's seen him. It's them, it has to be. He must have people watching our roads!" Al senior took a deep breath.

"Even so," replied Alvarez. "To simply walk into the village and through my front door? None of Basilio's men is that brave or stupid."

"So what are you saying, Grandfather?" asked Alberto.

"Perhaps some of our own friends are not quite as loyal as we might hope."

"It doesn't make sense though," said Al senior. "The people of the village might have noticed Johnny but half don't even know why he's here, and those that do, don't care all that much."

"Your friend Nolberto…he has had money worries of late, has he not?"

"Yes but…I've known him my whole life, we left the village together, he wouldn't."

"Maybe we should stop by his house," said Alberto. "Just to make sure."

"Fine," said Al senior through gritted teeth. "But I'm telling you he has nothing to do with this."

Al senior knocked on the door, awaiting the answer in trepidation. The door swung open, with Nolberto's wife, Maria on the other side, looking puzzled.

"Sorry to bother you, Maria," said Al, hoping he was covering his nerves with politeness. "Is Nobby around?"

"No, he said he was with you. He said you knew someone out of town who might have some work for him."

"Right, yes. Was that today? Must have got my wires crossed. Never mind!"

After shambling his way through a few excuses and a goodbye, Al senior turned stern-faced to his son. Alberto could see the dilemma painted across his father's face.

"It doesn't mean that it was him," said Alberto.

"No. But it doesn't mean it wasn't him either," Al said sadly.

"So what happens now? We can't just leave Johnny to…"

"I know. Damn it. I knew all this would end badly. And all for what, a prophecy? Some ancient gold? It's ridiculous! No doubt your grandfather will be meeting with the other old know-it-alls."

"And us?"

"I don't know son, I don't know. What do you think?"

Alberto shrugged helplessly. He was feeling more out of his depth than when he had arrived in England. What were you supposed to do in this situation?

Mateo couldn't have been happier. Finally, his father was playing football with him, there were no strangers, Paper

Monkeys or girls in sight and to top it all off, his father was letting him win.

That was until stupid smelly old crow-face, as Mateo was just brave enough to call him in the safety of his own head, showed up to ruin things as usual.

Mateo gripped the ball as Egecatl appeared seemingly from nowhere and glided eerily over the ground towards his father. It was a strange and rare sight, seeing the old man out in the bright sunlight of the day. Mateo was sure that one day he was just going to crumble into dust before his eyes, not that he would have any complaints about that.

Recognising the look on his father's face as Egecatl whispered into his ear, Mateo didn't bother getting his hopes up. He knew what that look meant. Grown-up business. Paper Monkey business.

Adelfo, seemingly employing the same stealthy tactics as Egecatl, sidled up to Mateo.

"I hear there are some more strangers in the old house at the end of the village."

"Maybe."

"I think we should go and have a look at them."

"My father says I'm not to go there."

"Well, he would say that, wouldn't he. Are you going to be afraid of everything your whole life Mateo?"

Mateo thought this was quite an unfair question, how was he supposed to know?

"I'm not afraid. I just don't want to get into trouble."

Adelfo pondered on this answer for a second, before snatching the ball from his grasp and making a run for it.

Mateo, surrendering to the fact that not getting into trouble had literally just vanished from his hands, made off in pursuit.

Laura emerged from a deep sleep, and for a few precious seconds forgot just where she was and why. Unfortunately, her mind didn't grant her any more leave of absence than that and the last few days soon rushed back in.

Looking over to where she had last seen Baz, it soon became clear what had woken her from her sleep.

"Where did that tray come from?"

"Some woman just came and dropped it off. Very nice of them to feed us, don't you think?"

"I suppose so," said Laura, a sudden rumble in her stomach reminding her that she should be in no hurry to turn down a free meal. "Doesn't mean I trust them."

"Of course not," Baz managed to get a few words out in between mouthfuls. "But finding out just what's happening is going to be much easier on a full stomach."

"Wait, did you see that?" Baz put down the tray, an act in itself which was something of a rarity considering the tray was still full of food.

"See what?"

"I could have sworn there was someone looking through that window…"

"Get down!"

Mateo pulled at Adelfo, who crashed down on top of him.

"Ow! What did you do that for?"

"Because they were going to see you," said Mateo wearily. "And we are not supposed to be here. I told you."

"And I told you not to be so afraid of everything. What happens when you grow up and be chief? Are you going to be so scared then?"

"I don't want to grow up to be chief! I just want to play football somewhere where there are no girls!"

"Well, if your father is chief that means one day you'll have to be chief. That's the way it is. My mother said so."

Of course, she did, thought Mateo. *She says everything else.*

"Well, what would she say about you getting me into trouble?"

Adelfo paused. It was not a conversation she and her mother had ever had. The point about getting into trouble was it was fine as long as her parents never found out.

"She wouldn't say anything."

"Liar!"

"Am not!"

It was then that a thought struck Mateo, a trump card that he hadn't even realised he was holding.

"Adelfo, if you think the prophecy is just a silly story, then why are you so interested in it? Why are you spying on the two strangers?"

"Because."

"Because what?"

"Just because."

"That's not an answer!"

Adelfo giggled at Mateo's naivety. "Do you know anything about girls?"

Mateo was taken aback. What sort of a trick question was that?

"I don't want to know anything about them. Especially you!"

Inside, Baz tried the door, to find out that it had been locked from the outside.

"Bollocks. We're locked in."

"What? Well, that does it. There's obviously something going on that they don't want us to know about." Laura marched over and tried her luck with the handle as if there was some strange skill needed to open it that only she had mastered. When it wouldn't budge, she kicked at it in frustration, before letting out a whimper and cursing herself for doing so.

"You alright? That's quite a heavy door. I wouldn't kick it if I were you." Baz said.

"Well," said Laura, now examining her bruised toe, "If I were you I *would* kick it."

"What? Oh right, I get you," said Baz. "Are you sure you want me to do this though? I don't want to cause some kind of political incident."

"I think we're a bit past that. I mean it's like if someone burgles your house, you're are allowed to protect yourself aren't you?"

"I should hope so."

"Well, someone's kidnapped us and is also most likely planning on sacrificing your friend. Don't we have the right to defend ourselves? Or break a few doors if we have to?"

"A few doors?"

"Well," said Laura matter of factly. "We're breaking out of this house. It's possible that we have to break into another one."

Baz began to stretch and roll his neck as if he were limbering up to compete at the Olympics. He took a few steps backwards, giving himself the longest possible run-up.

"Just have a quick check out that window, will you? The great escape is no good if someone's watching us do it."

Laura peeked at the window but saw no sign of spying eyes.

"All clear."

"Right then. Let's have it!" Baz roared as he charged toward the door, like a rhino who's rear end had just been on the wrong end of a hot poker.

Laura, if it was possible to feel sorry for an inanimate object almost did as the door collapsed under the charge of Baz, who flew through the now clear doorway and came to a stop an impressive few feet away.

Laura, who came running out carrying both their bags until she was relieved by Baz, spotted their best means of escape. Basilio had been quite literal when he had said the house was at the far end of the village, the fence which ran the perimeter of the village tapered to a point just behind the house.

"Baz, the fence!"

"Don't tell me you want me to run through that as well?"

"No, it's not that high, we can go over it!"

Arriving in front of the fence, Laura questioned her wisdom. It hadn't seemed that tall a moment ago.

"I'll give you a leg up," said Baz.

"Well, who's going to give you a leg up?"

"I'll manage. Now come on!"

Laura put her one foot in Baz's shovel-like hands and clambered onto the top of the fence.

"Are you sure you can get over?" Laura looked down at the other side. It looked soft enough, but then the fence hadn't looked that high…

"I'd jump down if I were you. I'm going to try and jump up, and it's probably best if you aren't sitting up there in case I miss judge it!"

Laura duly dropped down, a throng of pain shooting through her already injured foot.

Not that soft, wrong again.

"Baz, are you okay? Baz?"

Laura was aware of a sudden charging noise and self-preservation told her to put a bit of distance between her and the fence.

With a mighty grunt, Baz's hands appeared on the top edge of the fence and after a few moments of 'will-he, won't-he struggle', managed to convince the rest of his body to join them. More rolling off then jumping down, Baz joined Laura on the floor.

"Shit me," said Baz, out of breath. "Let's not do that again."

Laura nodded. "Fine by me."

She dug into one of her pockets and came out with a small compass. "All we have to do is head east, and we should come across Alberto's village. In theory at least."

"Well, 'in theory' has got us this far."

Laura laughed, partly in a hysterical 'what the hell am I doing' way but also because Baz seemed to be able to condense down any disaster into bite-sized chunks.

Laura held the compass up in the air. "Well, east should be this way."

"Then this way we go," said Baz, thinking that it was a good job he hadn't had a fitting for his wedding suit yet. At this rate by the time he got home he'd be able to knock a few of the extra 'L's' from his clothes.

Chapter Ten

"Oh good. You're awake."

Johnny's eyes opened as his ears acknowledged that the words came from the mouth of Lee.

"Lee?"

"Hello, Johnny. It's nice to be reunited with you."

"You've found your way to Alberto's village then? Bit risky, wandering around on your own like that."

"We're not in Alberto's village. You've been kidnapped, Johnny. As have I, in a manner of speaking."

"Oh. Did I pass out?"

"From the bump on your head, I gather someone made that choice for you."

Johnny put a tentative hand up to his head and felt the sore spot. Luckily his hair had cushioned a lot of the blow.

"So where are we exactly?"

"We're in the house of someone called Basilio, he's the village chief apparently. Turns out he had all this pilfered gold, and well…he's sort of been funding Easy Sell for years."

"And you didn't know?"

"These are strange people, Johnny. I don't know how but they got in my head somehow, sold me on a dream…" Lee paused. Morally he knew that he should tell Johnny that Baz was also in the village at that moment. But then again, Basilio had told him to withhold that information, and it had definitely sounded like a warning and not an optional request.

"But why would they kidnap me? This is something to do with Paper Monkey, isn't it? With my destiny?"

"They haven't told me much Johnny, only that there's going to be some sort of ritual. I think I might have gotten us both into trouble."

"I wouldn't worry. I mean why would they go to the trouble of getting us both here if they were going to do something bad?"

"I wish I knew, Johnny."

Fishing in his pocket, Johnny gasped in despair. "The bastards. Kidnapping me is one thing, but someone's nicked my sunglasses! Where is this Basilio bloke? Maybe I should have a word with him."

Johnny rose to his feet, and swaggered across the room, only to find the door was locked.

"Bollocks. So what now? Just wait around for this chief to come and find us?"

"It doesn't look like we have much choice I'm afraid."

"I'm not having that," said Johnny. "If I am something to do with this Paper Monkey, they could at least show me a bit of respect!"

Outside, the issue of respect was also being raised between Egecatl and Basilio.

"Show a bit of respect for the prophecy, Basilio. He has seen the symbol. He must be the one."

"That bag of bones? That waste of space? I find it an insult that he would be the one we are looking for! How do we know this isn't some trick? This 'Nolberto', why should we trust the word of a man who would betray his own village?"

Egecatl tapped his cane on the floor in thought as Basilio raged around the room like a pissed off hurricane.

"The prophecy says only that he would be delivered to us by an outsider. Nolberto is an outsider, is he not?"

"I suppose so."

"Calm yourself, Basilio, the end is almost in sight. It is only a few days until the full moon. Then everything will become clear."

"You are right, old friend. I should not doubt your guidance."

Egecatl placed a hand on Basilio's broad shoulder.

"Trust me. I will steer you on the path to glory!"

In the house of Alvarez, Alberto was once more sat around a table with his father and grandfather. He couldn't remember a time he felt so useless, so…young. The prophecy had always been there, always in the background. But now things were actually taking place that he never thought he would see, and doubts filled his mind. If the West were to kill Johnny, wouldn't it be his fault? If he hadn't gone to the student union that night if Johnny had never seen the tattoo…

"Don't blame yourself, boy." Alvarez spoke in that soft, reassuring tone.

"Sorry?"

"I can see it all over your face. You think that if anything happens to Johnny it will be your fault? You cannot help what has happened, the fates will be what they will be."

"Of course it's not his fault," snapped Al in defence of his offspring. "It's yours. You're the one who told him to bring Johnny here. Alberto should still be in England enjoying

110

himself and learning about life, instead, he's back here mixed up in all this mess!"

"My fault? Son, I can no more control these events than I can the weather!"

"Really? Well, it's a shame you didn't see any of this coming in your magical bloody fire!"

Again, thought Alberto as his father and grandfather went at each other. Again the prophecy comes between father and son. This isn't right. We shouldn't be fighting, we should be figuring out a way to find Johnny! A flash of memory of his first meeting with Johnny bought Laura back to the front of his thoughts. He had tried not to think about her, although that tactic had not bought much success. After all, why should he not think about her? About her smile and her laugh and the way he felt about her even when she was throwing things and shouting at him…where was fate there? Would destiny be so cruel as to bring her into his life and then snatch her away again?

"Will you two both shut up?" Alberto at first wondered who had shouted that out, especially as they had shouted it out in English. He then realised, as he was now standing up and had the stunned stare of his father and grandfather, that the words had in fact, come from him.

"This isn't right, any of this," said Alberto, returning to his native tongue. "This isn't about us, or what we all believe, not any more. This is about Johnny, an innocent man who we've all played a part in dragging into this mess! Now I don't know about you two, but I'm not going to be able to sleep at night if I know that poor Johnny has been sacrificed on some ancient altar and we didn't do a damn thing to stop it!"

"Well, well," Alvarez leaned back in his chair, his face for once unreadable. "It appears the son who was sent away to travel has found his voice. You are right of course. The prophecies of the West speak of war and death, whereas our legends have always been about peace and understanding. It is not right that we should be arguing amongst ourselves when a man's life is at risk."

"I couldn't agree more," said Al. "The question is what do we do?"

"The other elders think we should do nothing."

"How surprising."

"I, however, am not so old in my bones yet that I have totally lost the taste for adventure. Don't forget I was a firstborn son once, I travelled long before both of you."

"So what are you saying, Grandfather?"

"I am saying that your father is right. I have spent too long sitting and watching, listening when I should have been looking. I am the village elder, responsibility for the prophecy lies upon me. And I think it is time for action! I will er, have to speak to your grandmother first. Just to put her mind at ease you understand."

Al and Alberto shared a knowing nod. They both knew who the real chief was.

Mateo and Adelfo had watched in awe at the daring escape of Baz and Laura, luckily for them, they had been on the opposite side of the house to where the front door now lay splintered on the floor.

"I think we should follow them," said Adelfo. "I wonder where they're going!"

"No! We should go back, I have to tell my Papa!"

"And miss out on an adventure? Come on Mateo, it'll be fun. Don't be scared, I'll look after you."

"I am not scared, we are not supposed to go into the forest, it's dangerous! And anyway, how are we supposed to get over the fence?"

"The forest isn't scary, I go there all the time. There's a hole in the fence just down there."

"Since when is there a hole in the fence?" Mateo asked, horrified. His imagination flooded his mind with images of all types of mysterious creatures entering the village at night, mysterious creatures who liked to creep around in the darkness and eat little boys…

"Since I made one, oh please come, Mateo. It's so boring in the village!"

"No, Adelfo, no way, my papa will…"

"Your papa will what? All your stupid papa cares about is the Paper Monkey, Mateo, he doesn't care about you!"

"He does too!"

"Then why does he stop playing with you as soon as stupid smelly old crow face turns up?"

"Because…he's the chief and he's very important and children don't understand the things he has to do, but one day I will!"

"I thought you said you didn't want to be chief, Mateo?"

"Well, maybe I changed my mind. And if I was chief, there'd be no holes in the fence, and girls would know when to shut up!"

"Well, you can never be chief because a chief wouldn't be scared to go into the forest!"

And on that parting shot, Adelfo did what Mateo was realising was an all too regular habit and made a run for the fence.

"Adelfo! Adelfo!" Mateo felt his shoulders slump. Why did he even bother trying to fight it?

"Escaped?" growled Basilio. "What do you mean, they've escaped?"

"Well, Chief," said Rudolpho. "I was going down to check on them like you asked, and the door to the house was um…missing. They must have broken it down from the inside."

"And gone where?"

"Well, there are a few rumours that they went over the fence. Into the forest."

"Then they are lost, the forest is dangerous to those that know it well, never mind two outsiders. They will not be seen again," Egecatl spoke as if he was enjoying the thought that Baz and Laura might be swallowed up by the tress.

"Possibilities are not enough, I need to know! And what do you mean by rumours? Not one person saw them?"

"Well, the villagers are getting a bit jumpy about the Paper Monkey and everything. None of them wants to admit what they did or didn't see."

"Then they are ungrateful idiots and they do not deserve the glory that I seek for them!"

"That's not…the only rumour," Rudolpho looked down at his feet, had the ground opened up at that moment he felt it still would have been preferable to what was about to happen.

"Meaning?" Basilio stared at Rudolpho with a cold burning in his eyes that frightened Rudolpho in ways he couldn't put into words. He caught a quick glance of Egecatl, who gave a little shake of the head.

"Oh well, nothing really," said Rudolpho, stumbling over his words. "Just a lot of whispers I suppose."

"Perhaps a village meeting would be wise, to still the tide of idle gossip. The people will want to hear from their chief, Basilio," Egecatl suggested.

"That may be a good idea. Rudolpho, spread the word, I will address the village people this evening. And try not to get this wrong will you?"

"No, Basilio."

Outside, Rudolpho turned to Egecatl, exasperated in the old man's decision-making.

"Why did you not let me tell him about his son?"

"Because he has enough to worry about, and we can't know for sure Mateo is in the forest, children can be very good at disappearing when they want to, I'm sure they will turn up as soon as they are hungry, trust me."

"I suppose so," said Rudolpho. "I just would rather not give him another reason to dislike me."

Egecatl gave a crooked smile. "Oh, I wouldn't worry about that. It's long past time I filled you in on some plans of my own ..."

Basilio eyed the crowd that had gathered in the centre of the village. This was a good idea, it felt right. They would all see now, what he had worked so hard to achieve for them. His predecessors as chief, including his own father, had not worked like he had to bring the Paper Monkey to them. No, finally he would get the respect he deserved.

He strode out before them, Egecatl at his side.

"Brothers and sisters!" he began. "For centuries our forefathers have suffered the accusation of the heretics to the east, but no longer!"

The crowd murmured, in the way that crowds tend to do.

'Heretics?'

'Hey, my cousin lives there!'

'What forefathers? I'm the first generation!'

'Has anyone seen my daughter?'

'What about all the gold?'

'When are you going to fix that hole in the fence?'

Egecatl heard every stray sentence, every disbelieving and dissenting voice, every word mumbled under the breath, and revelled in it. Finally, things were coming together.

Basilio heard nothing but praise and adoration, his ego and twisted vision warping the words around so that by the time they reached his brain each had been transformed into undiluted acceptance of his rule.

"Tomorrow night, in the light of the full moon, we will take our human sacrifice to the temple of our ancestors and we will perform the ritual, and finally our god will be released to us!"

The wave of murmur died down as each person processed what he just said, and then like any good wave, swelled up and crashed down on the shore of Basilio's arrogance.

'Ritual?'

'What human sacrifice?'

'What about the gold?'

'Has anyone seen my daughter?'

Basilio was deaf to it all. In his mind's eye, the people were already bowing down and kissing his feet.

"The sunrise after next, the new era will begin!" With that he turned triumphantly away, sweeping Egecatl along with him and leaving the crowd to disperse, puzzled.

"The people seem ready for this, do they not?"

"Of course they do. You are a great leader, they trust you."

"And your men are ready? They know their parts?"

"Oh, they are ready, Basilio, you can count on that, they are ready. One question, what do we do with the fat one? This Lee?"

Basilio thought on it for a moment.

"He has played his part, we no longer need him. Take him into the forest and leave him there. If the fates are kind, he will find his friends and a way home, if not…well, that is not my concern. Now if you will excuse me, old man, I will spend some time with my wife, I hope she can benefit from my raised spirits. And if you run into Mateo, tell him to come home, it is getting late."

"Of course, Basilio."

Egecatl watched Basilio go and almost marvelled how easy this was becoming. Basilio had always been caught up in the idea of a grand destiny, and now he believed it to be upon him he seemed to become more deluded by the idea of power every day. That was, of course, if it all was a delusion, Egecatl joked to himself. There was always the slim chance that Basilio was right. He found himself laughing out loud as the thought cropped up in his mind. He was far too old to believe in such things, in silly stories for silly boys.

Lee couldn't remember the last time he had slept properly, but it felt like an age. He watched Johnny snoozing with some jealousy. How could he sleep so easily, and so peacefully with everything that had happened, knowing what might happen? The sleeping Johnny muttered something. Lee wondered what he could possibly be dreaming about that would appear to put him at such ease.

"Is this a dream?" Johnny asked the floaty shape in front of him.

"What do you think, Johnny?"

"I think it must be, seeing I'm standing in well, nothing, talking a...what are you made of, candy floss?"

The floaty shape twisted itself inside out until it looked flat, but it had a shape. The tail was a giveaway really.

"I am made of ideas, Johnny. Of thoughts and fears. Dreams and dreads."

"Paper Monkey?"

"If you like. My friends call me Bob."

"Right, only...well, I think this must be a dream really mustn't it?"

"Must it?"

"Well, I think if I really were having some kind of...I don't know, astral plane conversation or something, you'd have answers wouldn't you? Instead of just asking what I think."

"Sounds like you have all the answers to me."

"I wish I bloody did. I just wanted to make some music man, some good tunes. And now I'm...well, dreaming or hallucinating or having some sort of vision."

"Perhaps it's a bit of all three."

"Is that possible? And don't ask me what I think!"

"Anything can be possible if you believe it."

"Hmmmm," Johnny scrunched up his face and concentrated hard.

"Are you quite alright? You appear to be having an embolism."

"I just thought I could, well, I thought if this was all inside my mind I could change it, you know? Instead of us just standing here in this…this white nothingness."

"Nothingness? This isn't nothingness. Trust me, I've seen nothingness, and this? Not even close. No, think of this space as more of a…blank canvass."

"Oh right, of course. Standing in a blank canvass, possibly dreaming with a Paper Monkey shape."

"Is that so hard to believe? Wasn't so long ago that if someone would have told you that you were the incarnation of an ancient tribal god, you'd have thought they were quite mad."

"Yea but…at least it's something, isn't it? I mean it's flattering in a way, I suppose."

"Not for me matey. You think I want you to be cut open and bleeding to death in my name? No thanks."

Johnny sighed and looked around, or tried at least. Seeing as technically there were no up or down or any dimensions of any sort.

"So you're saying what?"

"I'm saying go and make your own destiny Johnny. That's what you've always wanted. I'd hate to see you come this far and change who you are. Get your own name up in lights, don't piggyback on someone else's version of destiny because it's easier."

"Right, right. Well, I er, I'll try and remember that."

"You do that, Johnny. Time to wake up!"

"Wake up, Johnny!"

Lee called out as Rudolpho and a few other men were manhandling him out the room.

Johnny woke up with a start and had quick look around to confirm he was back in a physical space.

"You need to stay here," said Rudolpho to Johnny as Lee was bustled out of the room. "He has to come with us. Very important."

"Right well...remember we have a contract!" yelled Johnny after Lee, and then felt bad for saying it. The dream or...whatever had just occurred was already fading fast from his memory, but he could just about remember the gist of it. All the kidnapping and staring into flames and being buffeted from village to village, he had almost lost sight of what he had originally come out here to do...if he was going to be stuck in this room, he might as well work on a song. Shame his kidnapper hadn't had the forethought to also steal his guitar, but he would have to make do.

"Where are you taking me? I demand to know? Where is Basilio?" Lee jostled with Rudolpho and his crew as they dragged him out of the truck.

"The chief says you are free to go."

"Free to go? Free to go where? I don't know where I am!"

"Anywhere as long as you don't come back here."

"But...this is a forest! You can't do this you know, I'll speak to the British embassy, I'll..."

Rudolpho laughed at him. "I'm sorry my friend, I don't understand what you are saying. Here." He threw him a bottle of water. "Enjoy your walk!"

Not for the first time in the last few days, Lee watched as people drove away from him, leaving him in the middle of nowhere. So now what? Take his chances in the forest and hope to meet civilisation? He picked a direction and begun to trudge aimlessly forward, feeling utterly hopeless as he did so.

"No," said Baz. "It can't be."

"What am I looking at?" asked Laura.

Baz guided her eyes, until they fell on a far away, but recognisable enough figure, ambling along.

"Is that…Lee? Do you think he escaped as well?"

"I doubt it," said Baz. "Maybe he was doing their heads in so they dumped him out here."

"Should we follow him?" Laura asked.

"Do we have to?"

"Unfortunately, I would guess it's the right thing to do."

Keeping enough distance between them so that Lee would be unlikely to spot the pursuing duo, Laura and Baz gave reluctant pursuit.

"I don't believe this," said Laura. "If this compass is right, and let's hope it is or we are really in it, Lee is actually heading east, and without a compass. How did he manage that?"

"I don't know. Perhaps this is a trap. Maybe they knew we would head east and they sent him this way to draw us out," Baz was surprised by his own paranoia but where Lee was concerned he was in no mood to take any chances.

"Well, there's one way to find out for certain," said Laura.

"I was afraid you'd say that. But I'm not going to be nice to him."

Lee had the horrible feeling that he was being watched. The smells and sounds of the forest had him locked in a constant state of anxiety, he was sure any amount of toxic snakes and spiders were eyeing him up for a tasty meal. Then he heard something, a noise he tried to ignore. Sounded like someone calling his name, but it couldn't be, no, he told himself. Just the wind playing tricks on him. However, when the wind then proceeded to call him some very rude names that all commented on his physical appearance, he decided that it was probably worth further investigation.

"Finally, I think he's heard us," said Laura as they got closer to Lee. "Now try not to punch him while I find out what's happening, please?"

Baz held his hands up in an innocent 'what, me?' pose.

When Laura and Baz appeared in Lee's line of sight he felt a relief that he hadn't experienced for a long, long time. At least whatever as going to happen to him, wasn't going to happen alone.

"Am I glad to see you two!" Lee rushed forward, arms out in emphatic embracing style.

"Easy on the hugs," said Laura, stopping him dead in his tracks with a stare that could have tranquillised a charging bull. "Would you like to explain to us how it is you were walking in the exact same direction as us, without a map or compass?"

"I really couldn't tell you. Basilio's men, they dumped me out in the middle of nowhere and I then I thought well if I walk the opposite way to the where the sun is moving I might just find the East village."

"Then this isn't a trap? Laura asked. He's not after us?"

"I'm afraid not, they don't need you and they don't need me, not now that they have Johnny."

"They what?" Baz lunged for Lee once again, before Laura bravely put herself in the middle of them.

"Johnny...he was in the other village and then someone took him and bought him to Basilio and there's going to be a ritual..."

"That would be the ritual when they kill him, would it? I knew it, I knew the second I saw you, that you were bad news!" Baz raged.

"I told you before, I didn't know what they were planning! Do you really think I would have brought him here if I did?"

"Well, you know what, you bloody did bring him here, didn't you?"

"Just give it a rest, both of you!" Laura said, still standing in between the two. "Is there anything else you heard?"

"No, no they didn't tell me much, they've had me locked away...I...wait, there is something. The ritual, the creepy old man, he told me the ritual would be on the next full moon...and I heard talk of an ancient temple!"

"So?" asked Baz, keen to do anything not to trust a word that Lee was saying.

"Temple?" Laura pulled out the map, which she hoped know was finally about to come into some sort of use. "Here, marked on the map, in-between the two villages...and right in the middle of the forest..."

"You think that's the one?"

"It must be," said Laura. "It has to be close to the two villages, or why would there have been an argument over it in the first place?"

"So now all we have to do…is find this temple. Can't be too hard, can it?" Baz asked.

"I don't know…this is a big forest," said Lee.

"Yea, well, hopefully," replied Baz. "It's a big fucking temple."

Chapter Eleven

Nolberto swung open the door to his house with a spring in his step that he hadn't felt in a very, very long time. Feeling the money in his pocket, he practically danced through the house, calling for Maria.

The voice that came in response unfortunately for him, wasn't hers.

"How much was it worth Nobby? How much did you sell your soul for?"

"Al? I don't know what you're talking about? Where is Maria?"

"She's at the bar with my wife. Said I could let myself in. Did you really think I wouldn't find out?"

"Al, I'm telling you I—"

"Don't lie! Don't you dare!"

Nolberto relented. He wanted the truth? Fine.

"You don't know what it's been like. Coming home to my wife with no money I had to do something!"

"You could have come to me, you know that."

"Yea and you would have loved that, wouldn't you? Bailing out poor old Nolberto again!"

"You betrayed me Nobby! You betrayed all of us!"

"Is this what you are bothered about? The prophecy? You of all people? Let the West have their silly little ritual, they'll dress up a bit, do a few incantations, and then when they realise that no-one's been smite, they will give up and let him go!"

Al shook his head sadly; could his old friend really be this naive?

"You don't understand. I know about Basilio, he's old school, he's a fanatic. He will kill Johnny; do you understand? He will kill him and you just delivered him to his damn doorstep! Do you understand that Nobby? His blood is on your hands!"

Al stormed out, unable to take any more. Fathers and sons, brothers and friends. Was there anyone the prophecy would not just leave alone?

"What is all this stuff?"

Alberto watched in fascination as Alvarez sorted through a variety of strange-looking liquids and dried out...well, he hoped they were dried out plants.

"Old remedies, very old. So old in fact, that no one had the good sense to actually write down the recipes. You'd be surprised how quantities can be mixed up when measurements are only passed via word of mouth through the generations."

Alvarez flicked a glass container containing a frothy dark liquid, which fizzed and made a whistling noise as though it was trying to prove his point.

"I'd stand back if I were you, boy. Some of these have been left to sit for a little too long. But don't worry. I'm sure it'll all come back to me."

Alberto watched his grandfather work which, despite everything competing for attention in his head, was quite enjoyable. The old man ummed and ahhhhed, scratched his head and poured things from one bottle to another, as though he were auditioning for the role of a mad professor.

"Can I ask you a question?"

"Well, you just did, boy, but carry on."

"Is there any part of you that thinks…that worries that they may be right?"

"Depends who you mean by 'they'."

"The West…this Basilio."

Alvarez pulled himself away from his concoctions with a sigh and eyed Alberto.

"Are you asking me if I am worried that if they kill Johnny it will unleash a vengeful and angry God that will slaughter our peaceful little village?"

"Er, yes. Pretty much."

"As much as I worry about the sun being snuffed out or the stars falling out of the sky. Say, did I ever tell you about a friend from my travels? An American man named Indigo Pete?"

Alberto had not heard of Indigo Pete, in fact as he searched his memory he could not recall one single occasion in which Alvarez had ever really spoken about his time in the outside world.

"No, I don't think you have."

"Ah, pity. Well, when this is over we shall sit down at your father's bar and I will tell you all about him."

"I'm sure that will be fun…" Alberto had no idea where his grandfather was going with this one.

"I will tell you all about how he lived for cards…well, died for cards actually but that is very much a tale for another time. The thing was, Pete always believed that though fate might shuffle the pack, it was up to him to decide how to play them. That way he could always remain in charge of his own destiny. Unless, of course, fate really screwed him on the deal."

That was it? No hidden life lesson? No nugget of wisdom panned out from the muck of memory? Alberto wondered if perhaps he was expecting too much from the old man. Perhaps sometimes a story was just a story.

"The point being…and don't think I don't recognise that look on your face, boy, is that the cards have been dealt, and we are not holding a strong hand. But we are not going to fold. We can still take charge of our destiny."

Alberto tried not to look puzzled. "We can?"

"Of course! When this is done, I will remind you of this conversation. Now perhaps you should go and find your father, I do hope he hasn't done something he will regret."

Alberto found Al, which hadn't taken too much time seeing as he was standing in the middle of the village square, staring into space.

"You found Nolberto then."

"Yea. You know he actually believes that Basilio will just let Johnny go? Like we could all shake hands over a beer and have a laugh about this whole thing. If only…"

"Well, Grandfather is busy mixing…whatever it is he's mixing. Doesn't smell great, I know that much."

"I keep thinking we should get more men…stack the odds a little in our favour but then I think…well, then I think I don't want to drag anyone else into this mess. Rumours are already flying; people are getting nervy. Even my regulars have picked up on it, I think. It's hard to tell really."

"Well, it sort of makes sense, doesn't it? If it's just three of us, I mean. Father and son and father and son."

"When you put it that way, I suppose. The stuff that myths and legends are made of. 'The mighty Pablez men, who did foil the fiendish plots of the West!'"

Al found himself leaping around, playing out a childhood swordsman fantasy.

"Did you ever hear about someone called Indigo Pete?" Alberto asked.

Al laughed. "So your grandfather gave you the card story, did he? I wondered when that would come out!"

"So he's not real?"

"Oh, he's real. But the old man tells the story much better than I ever could. Come on, we better get back before he blows up his house. Your grandma will never forgive him!"

"It is…beautiful. Forged by the gods themselves!"

Basilio held the blade up, examining it in the light.

"Quite possibly, Basilio. Its origins are…unknown."

Egecatl watched in hidden delight as Basilio was lost in the blade. The fool. Although he had to admit to himself, had he not sent Rudolpho to buy the blade a few days ago he could nearly have been taken in himself.

"It has been passed down through my family, waiting for this day." Egecatl almost had to stop himself from laughing at that one.

"Stained by the blood of our enemies…I can feel its power through my hands…"

Basilio had that look in his eye again, the look of a man possessed. Egecatl hadn't even counted on Basilio becoming this...fervent with the whole ritual process, but it was an added bonus. The more obsessed Basilio became, the easier it was for Egecatl to put his plans into action around him. There had not been much mention in the prophecy of a ceremonial blade, well, until Egecatl decided that it would be a nice touch anyway. After all, *if you were going to do this sort of thing you might as well do it properly*, he reasoned.

"I will ready the sacrifice," he said. "Then we will make our way to the temple."

"So it's agreed then," said Al. "I'll drive us as far in as I can, and then we'll make the rest of the way to the temple on foot."

"It seems the wisest course of action, in the circumstances," said Alvarez. "Basilio will only take a few men to the temple, our chances of stopping the ritual are greater there."

Alvarez began to fill his bag with the various substances he had been playing around with all day.

"I want you both to know, whatever you believe, that I am very proud of you."

Al said nothing in reply, giving Alberto the feeling that at least one of them should.

"Well, we'll try not to let you down. I just hope Johnny's okay."

At that moment Johnny was feeling okay, but that was only because he had been force-fed some dark liquid that was giving him quite the relaxed feeling. It wasn't like any intoxicants he'd had before though. He felt a lightness run through his body, and his mind suddenly became free of all worries. Even as he was tied onto a wooden platform and hoisted onto the shoulders of four robed strangers, he wasn't worrying. He looked up at the evening sky, at the crowning moon and the stars coming out to play, and felt a melody run through his head. This wasn't so bad. Perhaps he had been worrying over nothing. He closed his eyes and let the feeling rock him to sleep.

Night was creeping through the forest as Laura, Baz and Lee continued their trek.

Laura spotted it, although she didn't realise it at first. She had been looking for something that would loom above the treetops, it hadn't yet occurred to her that they might have to head down towards the temple. Without a word to Baz or Lee, she began to increase her speed, although she wasn't quite sure where she was getting the energy from to do that. It was as though the temple was drawing her towards it like a magnet.

Eventually, she came to a clearing, and then she saw it. The forest floor dipped down into a valley, and there stood the temple, as though someone had just dropped it there and forgotten about it like change down the back of a sofa.

Catching up, Baz was keen to find out what all the hurry had been in aid of.

"Laura is everything…oh wow. Do you think that's what we're looking for?"

"I hope so," said Laura. "Baz, look at that thing. It's huge it's…how the hell did they build that?"

"I don't know but I assume it was cheap labour. Lee! Over here!"

Stumbling his way toward them Lee too took sight of the temple and lost his breath in doing so.

"Oh…wow."

"Yea. That's exactly what I said," Baz replied. "Well, seeing as we're here, we might as well rest up a bit. We've got a good view. As soon as they show up with Johnny, we'll know about it."

Chapter Twelve

An hour or so had passed when Baz caught a glimpse of a crowd of people emerging from the forest on the opposite side of the valley. He could make out Basilio at the front, leading a group of hooded figures who were carrying a board on which lay Johnny. It had to be him. Even from that distance, the hair gave him away.

"What should we do?" asked Laura, for once unsure. The nature of what could happen very shortly was beginning to dawn on her.

"We can't risk them seeing us," said Baz. "Wait until they start climbing and we'll go up the other side. And we go quick," he looked at Lee. "Maybe you should stay down here."

"No arguments from me," said Lee. "I can er, stand guard."

After waiting for Basilio and his men to disappear around the other side, Baz and Laura made their way forward. The temple loomed before them. There was what could only be described as an inhumane amount of stairs.

Laura, concentrating on not letting her jaw completely drop off, found herself in a rare state of speechlessness. This thing...her mind told her off for calling it a thing. A miracle of a structure. Torches burnt bright every few steps, lighting the way upwards, a flaming runway to the heavens.

Laura could feel the history move up through her toes as she lay her foot on the first step.

Before making the climb, she turned to Lee, who was cowering behind the nearest available tree.

"Don't let them take Johnny again, okay?"

"I won't! No client of mine is going to get sacrificed!" *After all,* he thought as he watched her ascend, *that would be terribly bad for business.*

Johnny had woken up with many hangovers before, and all varieties. Happy hangovers, regretful hangovers, and more often than not, hangovers that made him grateful he couldn't remember the night before.

This, however, was an experience entirely new to him. Aware of being awake yet not having the ability to open even one eyelid to the slightest degree, Johnny could feel whatever potion they had given him still coursing through his veins. His ears, at least, were functioning though, they told him that people were moving about him, chanting in some ancient language Johnny had no hope of understanding. Strange scents and burning incense filled his nostrils. At least if he was going to get sacrificed he would be doing it with a clear sinus. A meek attempt at movement also told him that his hands and legs were tied, and from the slight draft kissing his backside he assumed that whatever clothes he were currently robed in had not originated from his own wardrobe.

Finally forcing his eyelids up like rusty garage doors, Johnny viewed a sight that no one should ever have had to have viewed after any period of unconsciousness, which was the full underside of Egecatl's crooked beak.

Johnny let out a noise so strange he couldn't quite pinpoint the body part of origin.

Egecatl smiled cruelly, which in his defence was the only real way he was capable.

"Don't worry. You will soon be meeting with any gods that you do believe in."

Johnny was sure that was supposed to sound like a threat, but the only gods he believed in were the gods of rock n roll, and the thought of meeting them in the afterlife didn't frighten him at all. Although…Johnny didn't want to die without making at least one world-changing album.

"I don't suppose you'd be willing to negotiate?" Johnny asked in sincerity. "I mean maybe if you just cut me a little bit your Monkey God might just leak out in instalments, and then we can all just have a few beers and a good old laugh about this I'm sure."

Egecatl let out a laugh that matched his smile.

"I'll let you in on a little secret. I don't believe that you are the Paper Monkey. But once this is done, and the Paper Monkey is still nowhere to be seen, the people will see what a fool Basilio is. He will be humiliated, and I will be the rightful village chief."

Johnny, who had seen enough films to know that whenever the baddie made a revealing monologue it normally meant the hero could escape, was severely disappointed to find that there was no conveniently placed piece of sharp material lying around that he could use to free himself.

"Couldn't you just have a vote or something?" said Johnny. "I mean, this ritual thing must have cost you a few quid, and it seems like a lot of hassle."

"I wouldn't expect you to understand. Basilio, he is consumed by the idea of revealing the Paper Monkey to the world. He wants to go down in legend. And he will. Just not in the way he thinks."

"Well, I'd like it noted," said Johnny, indignant, "that you sacrifice quite possibly the greatest musician not yet known to mankind."

"Be that as it may. This is going to happen. Best make your peace with it," Egecatl stepped away, addressing some of the robed minions that Johnny could see on the periphery of his vision.

Well, this was a fine old mess. Johnny squirmed a few more times, more for show than anything, and then gave up. Maybe the strange old man was right. Maybe he should just make his peace with it. After all, many artists only became revered after they died. Perhaps someone would stumble across his music, and word of his sacrificial end in the depths of South America would propel him into post-life superstardom. Then again, what was the point of being a rock star if you were too dead to enjoy it? *No, that's definitely not the way*, Johnny told himself. He had to stop feeling sorry for himself and get off this table.

Outside and a few hundred steps down, the rescue mission was in progress at the speed of the average post office queue on pension day.

"I swear," said Baz in-between breaths. "That these stairs are growing."

"It's all in your mind," said Laura. "Come on, we must be halfway up by now. Ow!"

Deciding to ascend on the dark side of the temple in a bid to avoid detection, neither Baz nor Laura had survived unscathed.

"Maybe we should have a little rest, Baz," Laura sat down on the step that had assaulted her already bruised toe. "And maybe we need a plan for when we do get up there."

"I've told you," said Baz, his voice taking an uncharacteristic edge. "Whatever happens up there, you get Johnny out of there and I'll take care of the rest."

"That's very noble of you. But I'm not sure I'm brave enough to tell Becky the wedding's off because I left you at the top of some ancient temple."

"My wedding. Bloody Johnny, I was going to ask him to be best man. He's going to have to pull off one hell of a stag do to make up for this."

Feeling inspired by the mere mention of his hopefully still impending nuptials, Baz began striding up the steps once more. The sooner he rescued Johnny, the sooner he could be back in the arms and at the dinner table of the woman he loved.

"The blade is ready?"

Egecatl unsheathed the ceremonial knife, and handed it to Basilio, playing the dutiful servant to the tee. Johnny, who could just then see the other robed figures standing in the doorway, thought he might as well go for one last bargaining plea.

"You do know that your elder bloke there is trying to get one over on you. Just told me so himself. Wouldn't trust him if I were you. But then what do I know? I'm only the human incarnation of your God. Don't feel the need to listen to me or anything. In fact, I think the Paper Monkey is speaking right now, and he says you should let me go."

Basilio wasn't listening. He held the blade up, eyeing his own reflection in the torchlight, trance-like.

"You have all done well, very well. The Paper Monkey will reward you all greatly I'm sure. And now…" he turned his glance down to Johnny and held the blade inches from his face. "I will free you from this prison, from this weak pathetic flesh."

"Oi!" said Johnny in retort. "If you're about to sacrifice a bloke, you could at least have the decency to say something nice about him."

Again, Basilio seemed not to hear him. Or at least if he did, he wasn't taking any notice. He stood statuesque, the knife staying unwaveringly still above Johnny.

"Egecatl…do you think I should have brought Mateo here? I think he would like to see his father fulfil his destiny."

"I think this is no place for children, Basilio. Now is the time."

Baz paused again, the top of the temple now well in sight. He placed a hand down on Laura's shoulder.

"All joking aside…if things get heated up there, I want you to do me a favour and run, okay?"

Laura put her protest into reverse as she saw the look on Baz's face in the light of the moon.

"I promise."

"One more thing."

"Yes, Baz?"

138

"I'm betting those ceremonial robes don't come with a cup. Any of them get you cornered or anything, don't you feel bad about going for the crotch shot."

"Oh trust me," said Laura with a grin. "I won't."

Baz checked the weight of the tree branch that he had hauled up with him as a makeshift melee weapon. "Okay. Let's do this."

Johnny blinked as the edge of the blade glistened a pointy wink at him. Surely in this situation, he was allowed to feel sorry for himself. He bet this wouldn't happen if he'd had a couple of good albums, maybe arranged a few benefit gigs, fed the world and got himself a knighthood. If he had been a national treasure and had been kidnapped and about to be sacrificed, the S.A.S or MI6 would burst in with grappling hooks and smoke grenades and machine guns and other paraphernalia that Johnny's mind's eye associated with a last-ditch military rescue. But none of that was forthcoming. What did come was a large, heavily sweating bald man, swinging a log and looking a lot like Baz.

"Baz!" Johnny shouted, equal amounts surprised and delighted.

Basilio shook out of whatever trance he had placed himself in and growled at his men.

"Stop him! Nothing can interrupt the ritual!"

To say Baz caught the guards by surprise was an understatement. Two were taken out from behind before they even knew what was happening, leaving the remaining three facing off against Baz, who was shouting a constant stream of obscenities that surprised even himself.

"Come on, come on!" Baz threw the cumbersome branch to the floor as one of the guards fancied his chances and charged forward, a mistake which he would regret for a long, long time as Baz's forearm smashed into his face, sending him spiralling to the floor, the hood coming up to reveal the now very bruised face of Rudolpho.

Basilio dragged himself away from Johnny and edged toward the action, as his three men who had already been taken down decided that the ritual wasn't as fun as they thought it would be and made a run for it.

Laura, who had hung back from Baz's initial shock and awe assault, crept into the corner of the room, hugging the shadows that climbed the walls. Unfortunately for her, Egecatl was doing the same. Long, cold crooked fingers grabbed her from behind.

"Not so fast, girl. How dare y-ooof!"

Instinctively remembering Baz's advice, Laura half-turned and swung her foot with as much force as she could muster in the direction of Egecatl's midriff. Judging by the sudden rush of air and complimentary groan that escaped from his mouth, she had made a full connection. Egecatl crumpled to the floor, wheezing like an asthmatic set of bagpipes. Laura stood over him and decided to have her moment.

"What's the matter? Didn't see that one coming in your prophecy?"

Johnny, still wriggling to try and free himself, pretended not to be too impressed by the large display of badarsery by Laura. After all, even tied up in a robe and seconds from death, he had to maintain some kind of cool as Laura made her way to him brandishing a pair of nail scissors.

"If you're done practising your action hero quotes, I would really like to be untied now," Johnny looked up as Laura began the job of cutting him free.

"Shut up, will you? The last thing I need is you talking why I try to rescue you."

"Ha."

"Are you seriously laughing?" Laura was starting to feel like leaving Johnny tied up for just a little bit longer wouldn't be the worst thing in the world.

"I knew you fancied me."

"If you don't want me sacrificing you for the crime of saying stupid things, then you'd better zip it. I mean, I would hate to slip and cut off any of your hair," Laura remained straight-faced as she spoke, and Johnny made a rare, wise decision to shut up.

As Laura cut through the last bond, Johnny slid away from the table and spotted Baz trying to swat away the remainder of Basilio's men.

"Baz! Mate, I knew you'd come. I never doubted it…"

"Later, Johnny!" Baz shouted over. "Now you run, you daft bastard, run!"

Johnny turned to Laura. "I can't, can I? I can't leave him here."

"Ideally no, but you're probably going to be more of a hindrance than a help at the moment…just wait for us at the bottom!"

Practically pushing Johnny down the stairs, and giving Egecatl a further kick as she did so, Laura turned back inside to see Basilio charge past his men to confront Baz.

"You…will die for this, this blasphemy!" he roared at Baz in his native tongue.

Baz stood, nonplussed and faced Basilio.

"Whatever you're saying mate, I'm guessing isn't polite. But you shouldn't go around trying to sacrifice people's best mates should you?"

"I cannot believe you idiots could not handle one man!" Basilio shouted at the two remaining robed villagers standing as he leapt forward, knife pointing outwards.

What happened next seemed to happen in slow motion, to Laura at least. Basilio and Baz met mid-air, like two rutting stags going in for the kill. The sheer force of Baz's bulk sent Basilio crashing to the floor, and that's when she noticed the blood.

Baz looked down in shock as the blood spread across his body and seeped through his clothes.

"Oh," he said, stunned as he dropped to the floor. "Bollocks."

"This way!" Alvarez pushed through the trees, leading the way with his cane. Al and Alberto followed him until they came to the clearing in which stood the temple.

They could just make out several figures fleeing down the stairs.

"Are we too late?" asked Alberto.

"I don't know, son. That one looks like Basilio but I can't be sure in this light. We need to get up there. Sure you can manage it?" Al looked at his father concerned.

Alvarez huffed at the suggestion. "Worry about yourself. I'm as strong as an ox."

"And as stubborn as one, father. Son, are you ready?"

Alberto nodded.

"Then up we go."

Chapter Thirteen

Johnny, lost in every sense of the word stumbled through the darkness, tripping as a stray branch snagged a piece of the ritual dress he had found himself in. With his slight frame thudding to the floor, the part of his mind that should have been concerned with self-preservation finally spoke up for itself. Unfounded optimism receded as doubt and realism flooded Johnny's consciousness for the first time in far too long.

"Peru, Johnny? Really?"

The words floated in the air, and for a moment Johnny felt as though the air might answer back, it certainly would have been easier than providing his own answer.

"Well, what was I supposed to do? The band left me. I was all alone. All alone again."

"All alone? They stuck with you through enough. They didn't leave. You pushed them away with your stupid dreams. Your stupid bloody dreams, Johnny."

"Dreams are all I've got. Dreams are all I've ever had!"

"That's funny. Seeing as Baz has travelled halfway around the world to save you."

"Oh shit. You're right."
"Now that, you dickhead, may actually be an epiphany."
"So what now?"

"Well, if I were you...and I am, I'd probably try and make it right with the few people in this world who actually give a damn about you."

"You're right. How do I do that exactly?"

"Who do you think I am, some kind of insightful talking insect?? Don't listen to your conscience, you Knobhead. He's even thicker than you are. But for a start, you should get out of that stupid fucking dress."

His voice was right. If he was going to do this, he was going to need his leather jacket. Johnny drew himself up, and prepared, for the first time in his life, to take some responsibility. Perhaps if there was some way he could convince them that he was not in fact, a human incarnation of their god than they would stop trying to kill him and he could get on with just being Johnny Rocket, a possible superstar.

"Joh-nny?"

A different voice this time, a smaller voice. It definitely wasn't his own. He looked around in the darkness, but couldn't see another soul. Unless of course...he felt stupid even thinking it. Had he ever really believed it himself? Still, he might as well try...placing his hands on the nearest tree to him, he leaned in as though he were about to go all French on the bark and whispered, "Paper Monkey? Is that you?"

From their hiding place behind a bush a few feet away, Mateo and Adelfo watched in the wonderful mix of amusement, confusion and fear that only children can do.

"Why is he talking to the tree?" Mateo peered through the leaves. The behaviour of adults was very much starting to disturb him.

"Maybe he's lonely," said Adelfo. "Your father did just try to kill him."

"You don't know that! They were just…you don't understand grown-up things!"

"I do too! I understand you don't take a big knife up to the temple unless you're going to hurt someone with it!"

"Sshhh! He's going to hear us! I am going to be in so much trouble…"

Adelfo rolled her eyes, something she was worryingly adept at for a seven-year-old. "Well, I'm going to call him again. I'll be his friend."

Wrapping a mouth around the strange-sounding word, she called out as bold as her voice would allow. "Joh-nny!"

Okay, thought Johnny. *That definitely was not the tree.* He turned in time to see two figures disappear away into the darkness.

"Wait!" Johnny called out in vain, managing a few steps before gravity and flora combined again to send him to the floor.

"I knew you were a wimp!"

"I am not!" Mateo swerved a tree root by memory.

"Then why are you running away?"

"You're running too!" Mateo protested, tired of having his fledging machismo challenged.

"That's different, I'm a girl. Girls can't be wimps, and to prove it, I'm going back."

She circled around in the darkness and went back the way they had come.

Mateo pulled up. He couldn't let her go back on her own, could he? Then again, it was her fault if she wouldn't listen, not his. He had tried to make her listen. As he wondered what to do, Mateo noticed that his legs had made their mind up quicker than his brain, carrying him back after Adelfo.

Catching up, he managed to grab onto her before she could reach Johnny.

Both crouching down, they could see Johnny lying motionless on the ground. Ignoring Mateo's silent protestations, Adelfo crept forward.

Johnny blinked as a young face appeared over his own.

"Joh-nny?" the face spoke. Definitely not the Paper Monkey, just a little girl. Still, Johnny, at least, had enough good sense left to realise that he could not be fussy when choosing allies at that moment. Pushing himself up onto his knees, he spotted another kid hovering behind.

"That's me. Johnny. Johnny Rocket."

Adelfo pointed at herself. "Adelfo."

"That's a nice name. Please tell me you speak English, Adelfo?"

The girl, looking confused, grabbed the boy behind her and pushed him in front of Johnny, whispering something that he couldn't understand. She then pointed at the boy and said, "Mateo."

146

"Can you understand me, Mateo?"

Mateo nodded.

"Do you know where my clothes are?"

Mateo nodded again.

"Can you take me there?"

Mateo nodded again. *Full house,* thought Johnny. He rose to his feet, still feeling woozy. Whatever they had given him had one hell of a kick.

"Then, er, lead the way. Please."

Mateo, still silent, turned and began to walk slowly away. Adelfo looked at Johnny, smiled with a shrug and followed. Johnny, who would have turned and shrugged had there been anyone to do so to, followed in suit.

Back at the top of the temple, Laura knelt down beside the stricken form of Baz, now framed morbidly in his own blood.

"Baz…oh God. Baz, can you hear me?"

Laura tried her best to recall the first aid course she had done at college. Recovery position? Didn't seem to be much good when someone's guts were spilling out onto the floor.

"Not as bad…as it looks," Baz mumbled weakly. "Go find Johnny."

"No way, I told him to wait for us. I am not leaving you, Baz."

Laura looked around for something, anything she could use to try and stem the blood flow. Grabbing a discarded robe and the remains of the ropes that had held Johnny, she tied the makeshift bandage around Baz's middle as tight as she could manage.

Now what? There was no way she was going to be able to carry Baz down by herself. Maybe she should go and find Johnny and Lee and together they could...

The sound of ascending footsteps from outside the temple's entrance snapped her into alertness. Perhaps Johnny had come back to help. Or more likely Basilio, come to finish the job. Gripping the scissors and standing over Baz like a mother bear, Laura steadied herself for a fight.

What came up the steps, was something of a surprise.

"Alberto!?"

"Laura?"

"You know this girl?" Al senior asked.

The Pablez men entered the temple. Alberto at first rushed over to Laura, and then halfway through this dash realised he wasn't quite sure what he was going to do at the end of it, so put the brakes on.

"Laura, what are you doing here? Who is..." Alberto noticed that he was standing in blood.

"Long story short, Johnny was about to be sacrificed, Baz and I came to stop it, Johnny escaped and then Baz was stabbed by that insane village chief and is now bleeding to death. Everyone caught up?"

Alvarez said nothing but unslung the pouch he was carrying over his shoulder and began to take out a selection of his home made potions.

"Can you help him?" Laura asked, fear quivering her voice.

"Perhaps," the old man replied. "The cut is deep but he looks strong. You did the right thing by binding the wound."

"Let's give your grandfather space to work, shall we?" said Al. "And perhaps you could introduce me."

"Laura this is my father, Al, and my grandfather, Alvarez. Father, this is my…this is Laura."

Al shook her hand. "You've come a long way."

"Yes, well, I read about the prophecy, and I knew how stupid Johnny was. We came to keep him out of trouble…oh God, we need to find Johnny, I told him to wait for us!"

"I will go," said Al. "I know the land better, Alberto, help your grandfather and get this man to the jeep, once I've found Johnny I will meet you there."

"Before you go," said Laura, "if you happen to see a sweaty, frightened man hiding somewhere at the bottom tell him to get himself up here so he can be useful for once. Oh, his name is Lee. That might help."

"Sweaty man, Lee. Got it."

At the rear side of the temple base, Basilio confronted Egecatll.

"How could this happen?" Basilio roared, eyes bulging with rage. "Your cowardly men have cost me everything!"

"My men are doing exactly as I told them, Basilio," replied Egecatl with a sneering smugness. "As we speak, they are heading back to the village to spread the word of your failure, of the shame and embarrassment you have brought upon our people. Of the money you have squandered that should, by rights, belong to all of us."

Basilio stood silent for a moment, the moonlight highlighting his angered brow. Of course, he realised. From the beginning, they were against him, they were all against him!

"Old man, you would betray me? You would anger the gods!?" Basilio asked, dumbfounded as his beliefs began to fall apart at the core.

"Oh, give it a rest with all that stuff, will you? No-one believes in the prophecy any more, Basilio."

"Then why were you ready to sacrifice a man? Tell me that!"

"I would sacrifice a thousand men if it would wake our people to what a fool you are!" Egecatl snapped back with venom, before taking a step back as he realised Basilio was still holding the knife, the bloodied metal pointing ominously in his direction.

Basilio felt a rage grow within him that he had never felt before. A volatile mix of betrayal and hatred spilt out from deep within, filling every inch of him with an anger he could not fully understand.

"I should end you here, Egecatl, in the shadow of our ancestors' temple. I should slit your throat and rid your toxic presence from my life!" Basilio spat every word.

"And then do what, oh mighty chief? Return to the village with my bloodied bones? Tell the people how you killed the village elder in cold blood?"

"They would understand. They would understand how you betrayed me!"

"They would drive you out, Basilio. You would be an outcast, a bad memory. Your son would grow up a pariah, ashamed to bear your name."

"My son? My precious Mateo? You would dare…!?"

Egecatl saw the look in the eyes of Basilio and wondered if he had gone too far. He had planned on goading him into humiliation, but not on getting himself killed in the process.

Basilio was too fast. Before Egecatl could issue a retraction of his last statement, Basilio had a hand locked around the old man's throat.

"I have a better plan," he hissed. "I drag you back to the village by your scrawny old neck, and you will tell the people what you have done, the sins you have committed, the web of lies you have spun around me. And then we will let the people decide just who they trust."

"Won't work..." Egecatl strained out a few words against the deadly grip.

"We will see, old man. We will see."

Descending on the opposite side of the temple, Al could just make out a figure hiding not very well behind a tree.

"Lee?"

"And you are?"

"My name is Al...you've met my son Alberto."

"Oh, him. The boy who left me in the middle of nowhere! I wouldn't trust him and I'm not going to trust you!"

"Well, you shouldn't mix with the enemy, should you? We don't have time for this!"

Al approached the hiding place, drawing Lee reluctantly from behind the tree of which he had somehow until then, avoided detection.

"Well, what do you want from me?" Lee asked.

"I want you to go up there and help. A girl named Laura asked me to send you up, Baz was stabbed."

"Stabbed? And Johnny?"

"Johnny has somehow got down here without you seeing him. Tell me, were you hiding with your eyes closed?"

"Not...the whole time," mumbled Lee.

"Well, I am going to find Johnny, you start climbing. From the look on her face, I suggest you do not piss Laura off."

Lee didn't try to argue any more, walking past Al and beginning the upward climb.

Making sure he had climbed a few steps before taking his eyes off him, Al turned his attention to looking for Johnny. With no sign and no conveniently fallen clues with which to track him, Al aimed for the clearest entry to the forest and hoped for a spot of luck.

Making his way into the darkness, Al couldn't help himself pondering on the nature of his connection to Johnny. A life spent resisting the prophecy, a life spent trying to believe in free will and the importance of choice, and where had it got him? Stalking through a forest trying to find a man who some believed to be a God trapped in human form. Al shuddered at the thought of it all being true, just to avoid how smug his father would be, if anything. It had to be all coincidence, didn't it? The idea that his travels, that the days of his youth that he treasured more than any possession he could ever have, the idea that all that was part of some divine plan just to bring a man to them made him angry, and more frightened than he cared to admit to himself.

A low branch that made him stumble reminded Al that a dark forest perhaps wasn't the best place to wander deep in thought. Looking upwards for a moment, the thinnest sliver of silver light shone through the treetops, illuminating a piece of cloth that hung ragged on a branch.

"Okay," said Al out loud, "I'll give you that one."

Shining his torch downwards, Al made out a hint of footprints impressed amongst the disturbed forest floor and followed them forward.

Laura watched as Alvarez tended to Baz. Alberto hovered around her, trying to keep his emotions in check. This was not the time to say what he knew he should say to her.

"What's he saying?" Laura asked.

"The chanting? I have no idea," Alberto replied. "Some ancient language only he knows...or made up."

Alvarez did not stop what he was doing but cocked his head in the direction of his grandson.

"So this is the girl. She's pretty."

"The girl?" asked Laura. "And thank you."

Alberto ordered himself not to blush, but it was too late.

"You told your family about me?"

"I didn't have much choice," said Alberto.

Laura turned her attentions back to Baz. Of course, she had hoped to find Alberto, but not like this. She felt selfish being happy to see him as Baz lay bleeding on the floor.

"Is there anything I can do...sorry I didn't catch your name?"

"Alvarez. And both of you, we need to get him to his feet. I have given him an ancient remedy that should numb the pain and stem the bleeding, but not for long. We need to get him back to the village so I can care for him properly."

"Will he make it?"

"I cannot say. Let us hope his journey does not end here."

Alberto and Laura took an arm each and with a struggle, just about raised Baz to his feet. Just in time, the wheezing

Lee clambered up over the final step and made a belated entrance to the temple.

"I heard...you might need a hand."

"Help us carry Baz down," ordered Laura. "We need to get him back to the village."

"Down?" Lee sucked in a mouthful of air. "Can't I get a breather first?"

"You had plenty of time to have a breather while Baz was fighting five men on his own. If you prefer, we could just leave you up here."

Lee looked around the interior of the temple and decided that it definitely was not somewhere he would like to be left on his own.

"Alright, alright," he said, taking an arm from Laura and propping it over his shoulder. "Down we go."

As he followed his young guides through the forest, Johnny allowed himself to take a second to actually think where and what he was following them into. After all, since he had arrived in Peru, he had tried to go with the flow, right up to the point of nearly being sacrificed, and now he was blindly following two strange children through the darkness. This, his newfound common sense concluded, wasn't right.

"Wait!"

Mateo stopped in his tracks, with Adelfo crashing into the back of him.

"Ow! Mateo, what did you do that for?"

"He said to wait."

"Oh. I didn't hear."

"That's because you don't understand English!"

"Erm, Mateo was it? Right?"

154

Mateo nodded in conformation.

"Mateo, I just, well, I wondered if you could tell me where we're actually heading because I don't really fancy running into that Basilio again."

"Papa?"

Papa? Well, I understood that, thought Johnny. And if this is Basilio's kid then he could be leading me right to him! I should have waited; why did I have to run? I should have waited at the temple like Laura said!

"Erm, you know what kids, I appreciate the help and that, but I think I'd better make my own way. I don't want to get myself or you, into trouble."

"What's he saying?" Adelfo asked Mateo.

"I think he wants to go on his own. I think…he might be scared that Basilio is my papa."

"Told you, he must have tried to stab him! Ask him!"

"I'm not asking him that!"

"Fine, tell me how to ask and I'll do it."

"No!"

Watching the two children bicker in words he couldn't understand, Johnny considered whether it was irresponsible as the adult to just run off and leave them. Surely it wouldn't be, they did seem to know where they were going, after all.

Al paused, did he hear voices up ahead? It sounded like…children? But what would children be doing out in the woods? Before he could get any closer, something came running towards him…Johnny!

"Johnny! It's okay, it's me, it's Al!"

"Al? How the hell did you find me?"

"Luck, I'm hoping on. Not destiny, not the gods, old fashioned dumb luck. Did I hear children's voices?"

"Yea, these two kids were leading me through the forest...then I just found out one of them was Basilio's kid and I thought...I am not taking any chances. I felt bad about running away but they did seem to know where they were going..."

"I'm sure they do, I used to play in the forest all the time when I was a kid, in fact, all the East and West kids did...until we all grew up and found out we were supposed to hate each other...Johnny, I need to get you back to our village, back to safety."

"Wasn't very safe the last time!"

"I know, and I apologise for that. But this time, I'm not taking my eyes off you until I see you on a plane home, understand?"

"Sounds fair enough."

"And Johnny...I need to tell you something. Two things actually. But first, we need to find my car."

"Look what you did, Mateo! You scared him away!"

"I did not, I..." Mateo stammered.

"You what? You scared of something else now?"

Mateo said nothing in response this time, he simply turned away and started heading home.

"Mateo wait! You can't leave me...I mean you can't walk on your own through the forest at night, you're too afraid! Mateo?"

He stopped, where she could just about still see him.

"I'm tired. I'm tired and hungry and I want to go home to my mother and if that makes me a wimp, then fine, I'm a

156

wimp. You stay here being all brave and having adventures if you want, but I'm going home, and you should too."

Without another word he carried on walking, leaving Adelfo wondering just how brave she was. The forest did seem a lot darker now that she was on her own, and she could do with something to eat.

Mateo paused, and looked back, he could just about make out the outline of Adelfo in the darkness. Hoping he wouldn't regret the decision, he ran back to her side.

"Mateo?," she asked. "I thought you were going to leave me."

"I was too afraid to go by myself," he responded. "But you are the bravest person I know Adelfo…and …you're my best friend."

Adelfo held out her hand for Mateo to take.

The two children stood for a moment in the darkness, holding hands and wandering what came next.

"Adelfo?" Mateo asked quietly, not sure if he was meant to break the silence but feeling far too awkward not to. "Don't move. There's a tarantula on the leaf above your head."

Adelfo froze from the neck down as she tilted her head upwards, just in time to see the spider drop towards her. With a shriek, Mateo yanked her towards him and they both ran as fast as they could until they reached the safety of the village.

"Mateo?" Adelfo asked sweetly as they sneaked back inside the village walls.
This was it, thought Mateo. No more being called a silly boy after that. Surely now, he was the hero. It was quite a surprise to him then, when what she actually came out with was "You scream like a girl Mateo."

However, just to add icing to the confusing cake, she then gave him a kiss on the cheek, before laughing and running toward her house. Mateo put a hand on the afflicted cheek. He definitely wasn't going to have a bath any time soon now.

Chapter Fourteen

"Nearly there," Alvarez pointed his cane in the direction of what appeared to be more trees, Alberto and Lee struggled under the weight of Baz, with Laura standing by in case of any collapses.

There had been a few sticky moments coming down the temple stairs, the odd slippery step where gravity had quite literally begun to pull its weight, but they had made it.

Waiting for them at the side of the jeep were Al and Johnny, who was now shivering slightly as the cool night air took advantage of his flimsy ceremonial ware.

"Baz, oh man, what happened to him? Is he okay?"

"Basilio happened. Stabbed him before he did a runner," said Laura.

"I knew I should have stayed…" Johnny looked in dismay at the bloodstains that now covered his best friend.

"And then Basilio would have killed you and Baz would have gone through this for nothing, now come on Johnny, help us get him in the truck," Laura felt her own exhaustion creep in as she spoke. If they didn't get in soon, she might need carrying as well.

"So what do we do about Basilio?" Alberto asked the question that everyone was thinking, but no one really wanted to confront.

"For now, we do nothing," said Alvarez. "He will go back to his village, no doubt, to lick his wounds, and we must do the same."

Basilio dragged Egecatl along, rage fuelling him. Arriving in front of the village to find that the main gate had been locked from the inside, which did little to appease his mood.

Standing on the other side of the gate, and sporting a pair of black eyes was Rudolpho.

"You will open this gate. You will open it and you will do it now!"

"I'm afraid I can't do that. The people have spoken."

"The people? I am their chief! The people will do as they are told!"

"Well, that's the problem really. The people are a bit fed up with doing as they are told."

Basilio gripped the bars of the gates, and for a second it seemed that in his anger he was about to tear them open, Rudolpho even took a step back, uncertain for a second. He knew what kind of trouble he would be in if Basilio ended up on the same side of the gate as him.

"Don't you see, Basilio?" Egecatl voice cracked as he massaged his neck, which still burnt with Basilio's finger marks.

"These people are tired of you. Tired of your…obsession with the prophecy."

"My obsession? Who has been guiding me since I was a youth? Any obsession I have is down to you, old man!"

"Excuses. I am a village elder, I merely guide the prophecy. You are the one who chose to abuse it. Who chose to squander our fortune, which has lain in our families...all our families for years! That was all you, Basilio!"

"No, no! It was all you!" Basilio said, fighting the truth now gnawing at him. "You yourself told me your own father sought out the man to bring the prophecy home!"

"And you destroyed his efforts. Driven by your desire for power. By your desire to rule, when you have overlooked your own people's needs for so long."

Basilio let go of the gates and allowed the red mist which had enveloped him to recede. He needed a clear head, he needed to think. If the old man had been playing games with him for so long, then he needed to be clever...

"And you, Egecatl? What do you gain from this? If I am no longer to be the village chief...then who?"

"Well, someone with wisdom of course. Someone who the people can trust to guide them down the right path."

"Ha."

Basilio cursed himself for not seeing it sooner. The old man had eyes on his title...for how long? he wondered. Had he planned this for years? Had all this been going on throughout his adult life? Through any move that he had made?

"And this wise man who the people will turn to, it will be you, would it? You have proved in your betrayal of me that you are not to be trusted! How can people trust a man who would live a lie for so long?"

"Because I did everything for them, for the village, for our history!"

Rudolpho, who now felt brave enough to get closer to the gate again, had to interrupt the tit for tat.

"Actually, Egecatl, Basilio has a point."

"What?"

"Well, the people don't want you as chief either. We all know what you did, and on top of that, you frighten all the children."

"You...ungrateful little...! I took you under my wing! I shared my plans with you...!"

"True," said Rudolpho. "Which is how I know what a complete and utter bastard you are. Dragging us all into a sacrifice? None of us wanted to do that!"

Basilio laughed at his former adviser. "How the worm turns, Egecatl! You gave the people a voice and they have used it to cast you out, so much for all your planning!"

"So who has the democracy chosen Rudolpho? You?" Egecatl sneered through the gate.

"Well, everyone's been talking, and we've decided we don't need a chief any more. We're all just going to...decide things together."

"And my wife and child, Rudolpho? Where are they in all of this?"

"Oh, right yea. Nearly forgot," said Rudolpho. "Your son was out in the forest all night but Egecatl didn't want me to tell you. Anyway, your wife took him and headed north this morning, said she was going to stay with her sister? She did not look happy."

"My son was what?" Basilio redirected his anger back at Egecatl.

"Oh don't look at me like that, Basilio! Can you be surprised? You never give the brat any attention."

"This was all for him..." Basilio felt his anger finally subside, as a reminder of what was really important washed over him, clearing his thoughts.

"Have I been so one-eyed? My son, my wife..."

"Are better off without you, Basilio."

Egecatl once again realised that he had said too much, but he was past the point of no return now anyway. If the people had turned against him then he may as well try and take Basilio all the way down with him...

"An hour ago I would have snapped your neck for such a comment Egecatl. But now I see through you. No prophecy is worth the loss of my family, and that is where we differ. The mistakes I have made, I made with them in mind. But you...you are just a bitter jealous old man with nothing!"

Egecatl snatched up his cane and thrust it through the gates toward Rudolpho.

"If you all think you can cope without me, then so be it. But I warn you, you anger gods more ancient than even the Paper Monkey!"

Rudolpho gave a nonchalant shrug. "I think we'll take our chances."

Egecatl withdrew his cane and gave Basilio an evil eye. "This is not over."

"For you perhaps. My destiny now lies in finding my wife and son, and making things right. Rudolpho, perhaps the people would see it that I may enter the village to arrange transport?"

"I'll ask around. Just, er wait there."

Watching Rudolpho leave, Egecatl could not accept Basilio's sudden change of heart.

"You don't fool me, Basilio. I know you better than you know yourself, the rage, the anger. You will not simply allow this to happen."

"And how much of that was down to you I wonder? The years of cruel whispers in my ear…what kind of man did you shape me to be, Egecatl?"

"Not an intelligent one, obviously. Plotting around you was child's play!"

"Intelligent enough to know what is important! Even if it may be too late…and even now you try to goad me. Why? We have already lost, both of us!"

"Because as soon as you were born my life became about standing in your shadow!" Spat Egecatl. "Always giving advice but never orders, but you…big strong Basilio, you were always destined to be chief!"

"If I could have seen what this quest might cost me, then I would have gladly given you the title, old man. Now I think it would be best if you got out of my sight. As you said, my heart is full of anger. Who knows in which direction it might burst?"

Egecatl slinked away, without another word. Basilio watched him fade away into the horizon, hoping he would never have to come across his crooked old features again.

"Basilio?"

Rudolpho had reappeared behind the gate.

"Everyone seems alright with you coming in as long as you don't try to…you know. Stab anyone or anything."

Basilio dropped his head, humbled. "You have my word. I would never harm my own people."

Al wiped the countertop of the bar for what felt like the thousandth time that morning. It felt good to get back to work, to some kind of normality, away from temples and gods and sacrifices. He knew it was far from over though, it had all gone too far. They were going to have to do something about Basilio…but not yet.

"Morning, son," Al addressed Alberto as he walked into the bar. Alberto took on a seat on one of the stools, a rare opportunity.

"Is it that early?" Alberto asked, looking around. Not one of the regulars could be seen.

"Even drunks have their limits. What's on your mind, son? Apart from the obvious?"

"I, er, I need advice. About girls."

"Oh," said Al. "What sort of advice? Because normally when teenagers go to university, they tend to pick up the…nuts and bolts of things."

"Nut and bolts? No, that's not what I meant!" Alberto said horrified. Thinking he would rather face down a thousand prophecies then discuss that particular subject with his father.

"Good. So what sort of advice then?"

"Well, it's just…" Alberto wasn't even sure himself. He and Laura hadn't exactly parted on the best of terms, and the relief he had felt when he had seen her, well, on top of all the other things he had felt… "Before I came back, Laura and I, well, it felt like we were getting close. I hoped. But I had already started to think about the fact I might never see her again and when I did…"

"You weren't prepared for it. Well, she is here now, and she travelled a damn long way to get here. I'd say you at least owe her a conversation."

"I know it's just…what if she didn't come back for me? What if she only came to help Johnny?"

"Well, son." Al put down the cloth, which by that point, was doing more harm than good.

"As much as I'd like to give you an easy answer, there really isn't one. You're just going to have to ask her the question."

"And if she shoots me down?"

"Then it'll hurt like hell. But it's all part of the dance son."

The morning sun christened the sky with bright rays as Alvarez took Laura on a walk around the village.

"It's a beautiful day."

"Indeed. So you like my grandson then, eh?"

Laura might have been offended by the forward nature of the question had it come from anyone else, but Alvarez just had…a way about him that put her at ease. A gentle nature, yet with a permanent mischievous twinkle in his eye.

"Well, I…it's complicated."

"Haha! Complicated? That's exactly what he said."

Laura found herself laughing too. This whole thing was ridiculous, wasn't it? She had only known Alberto for a few weeks, and here she was, on the other side of the world, strolling around with his grandfather who just happened to speak perfect English and who just happened to be the village elder.

"I don't believe in fate or anything like that," she said, "I just felt that I had to come. Especially once I'd read about the prophecy."

"You know, it could be said that it was your destiny to read about the prophecy."

Alvarez caught the look of scepticism in Laura's face.

"If you believed in such things of course. Ah, wouldn't you know, here comes the boy Alberto now. I shall leave you two to talk."

Waving at the old man as he departed, Alberto made his way to Laura's side, his heart thumping.

"So I see you've been given the tour."

"Oh yes. It's a beautiful place."

"Thanks. So…"

"Look I don't want you to get the wrong idea about me coming out here. I just, well, I happened to read about the prophecy, you see and then I knew Johnny would be getting himself into trouble and well…here I am."

Alberto tried to control the smile spreading over his face, although he knew it was about as much use as trying to stop a runaway train.

"You just happened to read about the prophecy, did you?"

"Yes. I read books about ancient South American culture all the time and I'm…oh bloody hell, Alberto, I'm lying. I was worried, alright? I was worried and I was annoyed at you and I just wanted to know what was going on. And…I'm sorry I threw that lamp at your head."

"It's okay. Good job I ducked though."

"Maybe it was your destiny to duck," said Laura through a grin.

"Maybe, maybe," said Alberto.

"So when this is all done, Alberto…are you coming back?"

Coming back? Alberto hadn't even thought about it, not properly anyway. Did he want to go back? Being wherever Laura was certainly seemed like a good idea to him, but no one had ever gone back after coming home. That was tradition, that was the prophecy. Wasn't it?

"I honestly don't know."

"Well, if you want my opinion, I think you should. I mean, if Johnny isn't actually the chosen one or whatever, then don't you have to go back and carry on looking for him?"

"I think I've had my fill of prophecy, Laura. Whatever I'm going to do next, I want it to be my decision."

"You know, Alberto, I think that's the wisest thing I've ever heard you say."

"Well," he responded, that smile now long past reigning in. "I suppose it must run in the family."

In the makeshift emergency room that had been set up in the house of Alvarez, Johnny Rocket kept a silent vigil next to the as of yet still unconscious Baz. He could barely look at the bandages, guilt overwhelming him so completely that he couldn't bring himself to even touch his guitar.

"Johnny?" Baz croaked weakly.

"Baz! You're awake!" Johnny leapt up in sheer relief.

"I'm not dead then, Baz said as he surveyed his bandaged torso. I've felt better though to be honest with you."

"Worse than that time in Benidorm?" Johnny asked with a nostalgic smile.

Baz laughed before a pain in his gut told him he wasn't ready for that yet. "Well I haven't got any feathers stuck you know where this time so it's a close second. Have I?"

"No mate," answered Johnny. "I don't think there was any drag queens in the ceremony. Alberto's grandfather patched you up, gave you some kind of homebrew medicine. Looks like good stuff actually, we should try and get some back through customs."

"Very nice of him." Baz said as he took a peek under his bandages.

Johnny had never seen Baz hurt before. Never seen him in pain, well, apart from hunger pains.

"This is my fault, Baz. You could have died because of me!"

"But I didn't, did I? Bit of rest and I'll be right as rain. I'm bloody hungry though. Do you know how much walking I've had to do? Too much. Still, couldn't let you get killed, could I? Not before you've had that bestselling album."

"Baz...we both know that is not going to happen. I'm..." Johnny muttered something that Baz didn't quite catch.

"Say again, Johnny?"

"I said...I'm no good. I...don't have any talent Baz. I was never meant to be a rock star."

Baz struggled his bulk into an upright position and gave Johnny a stern look, the kind someone might give a puppy that has chewed one slipper too many.

"You don't believe that, Johnny."

"Actually, for the first time, I do. Not sure when it came to me, sometime in between waiting to be sacrificed and being lost in the forest..."

"Bollocks, Johnny. I can't believe what I'm hearing. You mean to say I've dragged myself all this way, nearly got myself killed all to hear you give in? I don't fucking think so!"

"But..."

"But nothing! You signed a deal before you came out, didn't you? I tell you what's going to happen. We're going to go home, and you're going to record that album, and that's that, alright?" Baz lay back down, satisfied that he had got his point across.

"I…" Johnny, for a rare occasion in his life had nothing to say.

"Oh, and you're going to be my best man," added Baz. "Don't fuck up the stag night."

A knock at the door interrupted before Johnny could say anything further. Al's head appeared on the other side.

"Johnny? I think it's time I told you that second thing…"

"If he whines about not being a rock star give him a slap," said Baz, before closing his eyes.

Leading Johnny into the kitchen, Al pulled out a chair and pointed to Johnny.

"You're probably going to want to sit down."

Johnny did so, Al following suit then produced a photo which he placed in front of Johnny.

"As soon as you showed up I felt like I'd seen you before, Johnny. And I was close."

Johnny held up the photo, his eyes growing wide as he slowly realised what he was looking at.

"You knew my dad?"

"We ran in the same circles for a while, then one day he just disappeared. Turn it over."

Johnny looked at the words, and though he couldn't read Spanish, two words needed no translation.

"Tommy Rocket. I can barely remember him, I…"

Al waited patiently for Johnny to put the dots together.

"He had the tattoo? Which means that…" The realisation finally lit up Johnny's brain like a lightning bolt from the heavens. "I was just drawing from memory? Oh bollocks, I was just drawing from memory…so…I'm not the Paper Monkey?"

"I don't think so, no."

A normal person in this circumstance may have been bogged down by guilt at this point. Riddled with self-doubt and paranoia by the ridiculous circumstances that they had found themselves in, it could have cracked a sane man. But this, after all, was no normal man. This was Johnny Rocket.

"This is fantastic! Mega! Amazing!" Johnny leapt up from his seat and began the process of merrily jigging across the kitchen.

Al watched in amazement. This was definitely not the reaction he had been expecting.

"You are happy about this?"

"Happy? I'm relieved! Do you know how much pressure this takes off of me? Baz was right, I can get on with my own destiny now, and make my music!"

"And your father? Aren't you angry at him?"

"Nah. His loss."

Al was astonished. How could anyone go from being nearly sacrificed because of a coincidence to bouncing around in elation?

"Right, well. As long as you're happy…"

Chapter Fifteen

"It is time," Alvarez addressed the unlikely team of people that fate had brought together. At least that's what had brought them together in his mind. After much debate, he had decided to do what no elder of the village had done for generations. It was time to go to the West and speak to the people. They could not go on for another generation, not after recent events.

"I'm still not sure about this," said Al, who had protested the idea from the beginning. "You think Basilio will just invite you in for a drink?"

"Several little voices tell me that Basilio is no longer there, he was seen travelling north. As for Egecatl, I can only assume that for now, he has crawled under the rock from which he came."

"So, you think he'll be back to cause more trouble?"

"Oh, I have no doubt my boy. But that's a worry for another day."

"I have to say," said Lee. "I really do not fancy going back to that place."

"If we're going," said Baz, still not trusting Lee. "Then you're going."

Johnny, who had stayed mostly silent during the debate, piped up with a thought.

"I think it's a good idea. Spread the love! I could always play them a song."

"Perhaps I should do all the talking." From anyone else, it might have sounded like a putdown, but Alvarez's smile could have sugar-coated the harshest of barbs.

Rudolpho was repairing a hole in the fence when he heard the commotion. He'd definitely remember the people saying they didn't need, or want a village chief any more. What he hadn't realised was that people still wanted someone to fix things and make decisions, and at the moment all those things seemed to be falling to him.

Making his way to the village gates, he soon saw what all the hubbub was about. Various village people were gathered in front of the gate. The murmuring rose up again and hit Rudolpho as he made his way to the front of the crowd.

At the other side of the gate was stood an old man and behind him, a group of people, one of whom made Rudolpho wince as he remembered the last time he had encountered the man-mountain of Baz.

"Hello friend," said the old man. "I am Alvarez, chief elder of the East. Any chance you'd like to let us in?"

"Well, that's not really up to me. Apparently," Rudolpho turned to the people behind him.

"What do you think? Should we let them in?" It was an act that Rudolpho regretted instantly, as the amassed voice seemed to fuss and fret back at him.

'Basilio would never stand for this!'

'Why's he asking us for? Didn't we put him in charge?'

'Seriously, where's all the gold?'

Alvarez recognised the look on Rudolpho's face.

"Looks like you have your hands full. It's alright, we can wait. It's a lovely day after all."

Rudolpho looked at the people on both sides of the gate and decided that he couldn't be worse off for letting them in.

"Hang on. I'll get the keys."

Moments later, Rudolpho led Alvarez and company through to the centre of the village. The village people who had gathered followed as though caught in the mind-controlling melody of a pied piper.

"People of the West!" Alvarez practically sang out his words. "I am Alvarez, chief elder of the East. Our prophecies tell of a day when we would have peace between us when one man would bring us together! This is that day! And this…" Alvarez grabbed Johnny and thrust him forward, much to his surprise, "…is that man."

"I am?" asked Johnny. "But the photo? I'm not the Paper Monkey!"

"Perhaps not. But you are here, and Basilio and Egecatl and their warring ways are not. Prophecy fulfilled."

The people seemed unsure. It was all well and good saying that there was a new age of peace, but how could they know for sure? Surely there had to be something to seal the deal.

Al, who had spotted the uncertainty had an idea. If this couldn't bring their peoples together than nothing could.

"To mark this…historic day. I'd like to offer you all half-price drinks at my bar. All welcome!"

That nearly had them, nearly. Al could see it. He just needed something to sweeten the deal…

"And the first drink is on the house!"

Later that evening after the two villages had been getting acquainted at Al's bar, Alvarez left the party early. His heart filled with renewed faith in his people and his beliefs, he made his way home on a tide of goodwill. Out of the corner of his eye, he caught something slither past him in the darkness, and then before he knew what was happening, felt a blade at his throat.

"You think you've won, don't you?" The desperate voice of Egecatl whispered in his ear.

Alvarez did what he always did, and laughed.

"Won? This is not about winning. Look at the joy on the people's faces. New brothers, new sisters, new friends. The people are happy, Egecatl. Both of our peoples."

"They do not deserve to be happy! They are treacherous sheep!" Egecatl shouted to the sky in frustration.

"Well, I have to disagree. So do you have a plan? Or are we going to stand out here all my night, because I don't want my dinner getting cold."

Egecatl pulled the knife away and spun around so that he was now facing Alvarez.

"You think I won't do it? Nothing could bring me greater joy than wiping that smirk off of your face!"

"Joy? I don't think you understand the word. Oh, and by the way, there's someone standing behind you."

"Do you really think that I would…" Egecatl collapsed to the floor as something heavy hit him from behind.

Lee stood triumphantly over the crumpled form of Egecatl.

"Nasty little chap isn't he?"

"Just a bit. Good timing."

"Came out for some air...and he really had that coming. What should we do with him?"

Alvarez gave Egecatl a tap with his cane to make sure that he was out.

"Go back to the bar and get Rudolpho. It's up to them what they want to do with him."

"And you?"

"I'm going home for my dinner. Good night."

The next morning, with the entire two villages nursing sore heads, Alberto found himself waking with a dilemma that still plagued his mind.

Someone was singing, badly.

"Morning, Johnny."

"It's a song I'm working on, in case you were wondering. Laura tells me you haven't made up your mind yet."

"No, not quite, I..." Alberto couldn't quite believe what he was about to ask Johnny, but he had asked everyone else so he thought he might as well.

"What do you think I should do?"

"Well, that depends doesn't it?" Johnny replied in earnest.

"On what?"

"On whether you have a good reason to stay or not. I mean...there's peace between the villages now, isn't there? And if you have something or someone to go back for, well...you've got to see where that takes you. Trust me, you'll regret it otherwise."

"Is that from a song as well?" Alberto asked.

Johnny whipped out his notebook. "Not yet, but it's not the worst idea ever." He made a few scribbles and returned the notebook to his pocket.

"So what about you, Johnny? When you go back I mean...what will you do?"

"Well, as it stands, I'm still not a rockstar, am I? The dream hasn't changed. I've just gotten...side-tracked a bit."

"So you're still going to make your music?"

Johnny answered with a smile. "I'm going to try."

Chapter Sixteen

Laura stared at the textbook, trying to convince herself that she was actually interested in doing any work. It had been two months since herself, Baz, Johnny and Lee had returned from Peru. Two months since they all dropped back into normality. Becky had asked her to join her team of bridesmaids, which had been a nice gesture. Laura pulled out the wedding invitation from a drawer and read it to herself again. 'Plus guest'. There was only one person she wanted to take and he was…well, he'd made his choice, hadn't he? She just had to live with that…she had been so sure though. That last day when they'd all left…she thought he would come back.

A bleep from her phone lulled her into false hope, as it had done several times over the last fortnight. It was just Baz, inviting her to a gig at the Brunswick Cross. She didn't feel like going but she couldn't just sit around moping, could she? That wasn't her after all. Replying with false joviality, she turned her attention back to her books. It was no good. They just seemed so boring now…

It had been the easiest decision he'd made in a long, long time, thought Lee as he signed the paperwork. Whilst he had been gone, a big-time label had made an offer for his struggling company, and he couldn't have been happier to hand it over. Some of the money he would send back to Peru, the rest he would keep to invest in a new company. One that put its faith in unheard-of artists who had a dream, a vision. A destiny. Starting with a certain Johnny Rocket of course.

Taking in the view from his office for the final time, he took a deep breath and felt a freedom he hadn't felt in well…he couldn't even remember when. Plus, he felt lighter. Not just physically, although his trousers weren't so tight now, he felt a lightness in his soul, as though a terrible burden had been lifted from him. There was just one more thing he had to take care of. He leant down and pushed a button on his desk.

"Susie, could you come in here for a second please?"

"Yes, Mr Jones."

A moment later Susie duly appeared.

"So, I've signed all the paperwork. The deal should go through on Monday."

"Very good, Mr Jones."

"I have, of course, insisted that all my staff should keep their jobs."

"Very good, sir."

"All the staff except you, of course."

Susie stuttered slightly, before regaining her composure. "Well, that's…times are hard."

"Indeed. Which is why I need someone in my new venture I can trust, someone hardworking and reliable."

"I imagine you do, sir."

"I'm talking about you, Susie. I would like you to come and work with me. In fact, I'd like you to run the show really.

Give me a chance to be hands-on with our artists. What do you think?"

Lee caught the hint of a blush.

"That sounds very good, sir."

"Excellent. Well, seeing as this is your last day here, why don't you take the rest of the day off."

"Thank you, sir."

"You're more than welcome, and please just call me Lee,"

"Yes, si- Lee."

Lee watched her leave the room and leaned back in his chair. Things were looking up.

It was a busy night at the Brunswick Cross, as busy as it got without tear gas being involved anyway.

Johnny waited nervously in the cupboard that doubled up as backstage.

Staring at boxes of cheese and onion crisps, pork scratchings and some wine that shared more in common with de-icer than a vineyard, Johnny paused to think about his first solo gig. This was what it was all about though, wasn't it? Starting small, after everything he had been through he realised that much now. He took a peek through the door and spotted Baz and Becky sharing a table with Joe and Sponge. The band was back together in spirit at least. Over at the bar, he spotted Laura sitting alone. Ordinarily, he might have felt sorry for her, but ordinarily, he wouldn't have known who was about to walk through the pub's entrance at any moment.

Laura sat at the bar, nursing a drink. Buster Head smiled at her, which she was sure he was attempting to do in a friendly way but when Buster Head smiled, it was physically impossible for his face to look friendly. It was the smile a pirate might give before making you walk the plank.

"Excuse me, is this seat taken?"

Laura was so wrapped up in her thoughts she didn't even register the voice, her mind merely acknowledged the words.

"I wouldn't bother if I were you," she replied, without even turning around.

"Oh, that's a shame. I could do with sitting down. I've come a long way."

This time, it hit home straight away.

"Alberto?"

The Peruvian grinned broadly. "In the tattooed flesh!"

"But I thought…wait, you know what? If you think you can just swan in here after leaving me to wait for the past few months, then you can just…"

"Just what?"

"Well, you can at least start by buying a girl a drink."

Alberto took his seat on the stool next to Laura.

"That I can do. You know what? I might even have one myself…"

Johnny watched the scene at the bar and with a nod to Buster, decided it was time to make an appearance. Strutting onto the stage with his guitar in hand, he stood behind the mike and gripped it tightly. Waiting for a moment for the applause to…happen, Johnny shook this off and addressed the crowd.

"This is my new song. It's called…The Legend of Paper Monkey…"

Later, to celebrate the fact that the pub survived the gig without having to call out a glazier, Buster allowed Johnny and his 'crew' to have a lock-in.

"I have to hand it to you, John, that wasn't half bad," said Joe. "I mean, compared to what you…" He stopped short as Baz shot him daggers.

"Yea mate," Sponge chipped in. "I'm almost sorry we didn't come to Peru. Until I saw Baz's scar, that is. You do know next time you go on holiday your travel insurance is gonna be a nightmare to get."

"It's even bigger now," smiled Baz. Becky patted his stomach, "I may have overdone it a little bit with the comfort food."

Alberto watched as the old friends laughed, drank and made a lot of jokes at Johnny's expense. He looked at Laura, who smiled at him in a way that made him glad at any kind of prophecy that had brought them together.

Johnny let everyone get a certain level of drunk before he made his final announcement. He couldn't be sure how it was going to go down, but he had already made his mind up.

"Look, everyone. I'm glad you've all had a good time, and it's great to see everyone together. If I've learnt anything, it's that…" He tried not to well up as he looked at Baz.

"It's that I've never really appreciated what I've got. Too much time chasing what I thought I needed, I started to believe all that Paper Monkey stuff. So I've been reading, doing some research. At the library. And I found this book," Johnny produced a leather-bound old book which landed with a meaningful thud, partly spilling Sponge's pint and leaving him calculating what percentage of his three-pound-fifty

Johnny now owed him. The rest of the group looked at Johnny in silence. Had it happened, had Johnny Rocket finally grown up and removed his head from the clouds? That was until Laura noticed the title of the book and said it out loud in a hushed, more than slightly concerned tone.

"Musical Legends and Myths: A History."

She looked across to Baz who had also seemingly clocked the title and was switching his face from 'Beer and Food Baz happy' to 'What is he up to now?'

Johnny could see the looks he was getting and decided to just plough through.

"I know it was crazy, thinking that I could be the *actual* Paper Monkey. That was never really my destiny. But I found this, the story of the first guitar. Apparently, whoever plays it would be the greatest musician in the world!"

As he had months previously when he had signalled his intent to go to Peru, Johnny let the words hang in the air and watched as his friends suffered a collective brain freeze.

Buster Head, who had shuffled over to collect glasses and finally call time broke the bubble of silence.

"Bloody hell, Johnny. Just give it a rest, son, will you?"

Johnny paused, and then found himself exploding with laughter.

"I got you! I got all of you!" Johnny sat back down and took a triumphant swig of beer. He closed the book and watched as his friends, old and new all laughed with him rather than at him. It was a good feeling, a real feeling. Still, he slid a plectrum onto page twenty-eight just in case. After all, destiny was destiny…

The End

Epilogue

Not too long after, someone else came across a copy of 'Musical Legends and Myths: A History'. Most definitely a man, most probably named Derek. He looked like a Derek anyway. One day Derek was digging in a field, not for anything in particular. That way, there was no way he could be disappointed if he didn't find the thing that he wasn't even looking for anyway, and anything he did find was a bonus. Derek was so used to not finding the thing that he wasn't even looking for anyway, that when his little foldable shovel hit something that wasn't an earthworm's bedroom, he wasn't quite sure how to react. Cautiously, he knelt down and brushed away a bit of soil, which revealed a corner. His heart skipped a beat. A corner. An actual corner! Of course, a corner, in general, wouldn't be all that exciting, but when you had dug up as many used condoms and dead hedgehogs as Derek had (sometimes at the same time, which had posed several questions that Derek could not answer) it was exciting times indeed. A corner meant sides, and possibly even…more corners! Derek sat back on the grass, a little giddy with the find. Taking a calming sip from his flask of tea, Derek dug on.

Half an hour later, Derek had uncovered the whole object. There had been sides all right, and corners. Three more of the things! It was some kind of wooden chest, which was in quite a good condition, seeing as it had been underground for however long. Derek's hand hovered over the lid. There was no lock, but something held him back. He had the sudden urge to look around, paranoia creeping over him. Fear that someone was hiding behind a tree, ready to steal his find and take the glory for themselves. Bollocks to that, thought Derek as he tried his best to stare out a sheep in a neighbouring field that was looking a little too closely for his liking. All that spiky latex would not have been for nothing. Derek lifted the lid, and there he saw it. The thing that he hadn't even been looking for anyway, for the last twenty years was staring him in the face. He then did something that was even rarer than finding treasure, Derek smiled. A proper smile. A toothy, ear-to-ear, face aching smile. He might even get find of the year at his treasure hunters club, then it would be his name up on the wall, and that smarmy git Fred could take his Roman coins and stick them where the sun didn't shine. Putting on a pair of gloves, Derek carefully lifted the item from the chest. It seemed to be impossible, and given its age, the item was hardly in pristine condition but there was no mistaking. It was definitely a guitar…